Gone with the Wine...

Gone with the Wine…

Doug Pike

The Wine Appreciation Guild
San Francisco

Gone with the Wine: The Wine Cartoons of Doug Pike
Copyright © 2009 by Doug Pike

Published by:
The Wine Appreciation Guild
360 Swift Avenue
South San Francisco, CA 94080
(650) 866-3020
www.wineappreciation.com

Book Design: TIPS Technical Publishing, Inc.

Cover Design: Diane Spencer Huma

Library of Congress Cataloging-in-Publication Data

Library of Congress Control Number: 2009925024

ISBN 978-1-934259-05-4

Printed in Korea

For Beth, Dan, Mom & Dad

Contents

Foreword

For quite some time now subscribers to my website, eRobertParker.com, have gotten a regular chuckle or belly laugh from Doug Pike's weekly Wine Cartoon of the Week. Doug has a real feel for the psyche of the serious wine nut (and his/her long suffering spouse) and never fails to poke fun at them with a deft hand and his own trademark brand of humor. I'm sure wine lovers all over the world will enjoy this collection of cartoons from Doug.

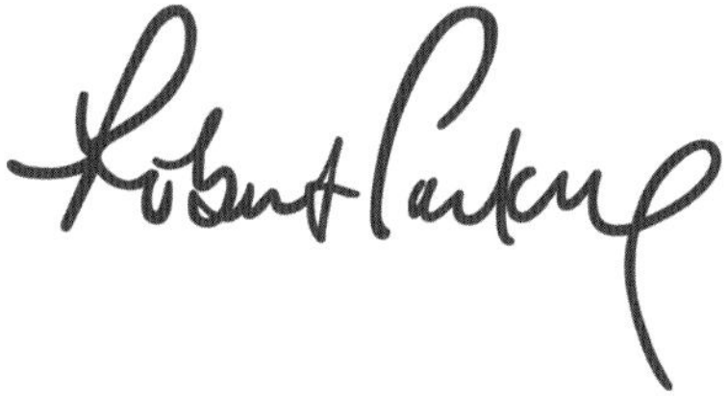

Introduction

You never hear about a famous New York auction house hosting a beer auction. And you never hear about millions of dollars being speculated on beer futures. Lastly, you will never hear the average guy on the street being referred to as "Joe 750ml." Why?

It's because, despite years of expensive advertising campaigns, wine is still considered the beverage of the elite (at least in the U.S).

And, since cartoonists love to attack symbols of authority and elitism, either directly or indirectly, wine is a prime target.

Think about how, where, and why wine is used in our culture. It's used to christen ships; it's used in religious ceremonies; it's used by heads of state to toast one another, and it's served at lavish, Washington banquets. In movies, the serving of wine or Champagne is frequently associated with a special moment. Its presence helps establish the sophistication of the individual ordering or consuming it. Even at a family dinner, held at a neighborhood restaurant, someone simply has to suggest ordering a bottle of wine and a sudden hush falls over the group, as if the winning Powerball numbers are about to be announced. Eyebrows rise. Will the proper wine be ordered? Will whoever takes on the overwhelming responsibility of tasting the wine do so without embarrassing himself, or triggering World War Three?

This is the kind of stuff a cartoonist absolutely drools over; situations ripe with enough raw material to keep the ink flowing all winter. And the astounding part is that it's all over fermented grape juice. What could be more bizarre? Not much. And I'm thankful for it, because this lunacy inspired me to write and draw these cartoons.

Wine really is a wonderful beverage that should be enjoyed without a lot of hype. Making light of all the various aspects of wine ostentation helps disarm it. And that in turn helps bring it into people's lives so they won't miss out on its benefits.

Cheers!

Doug Pike

1

The Merchant of Vinous:
The Retail Experience

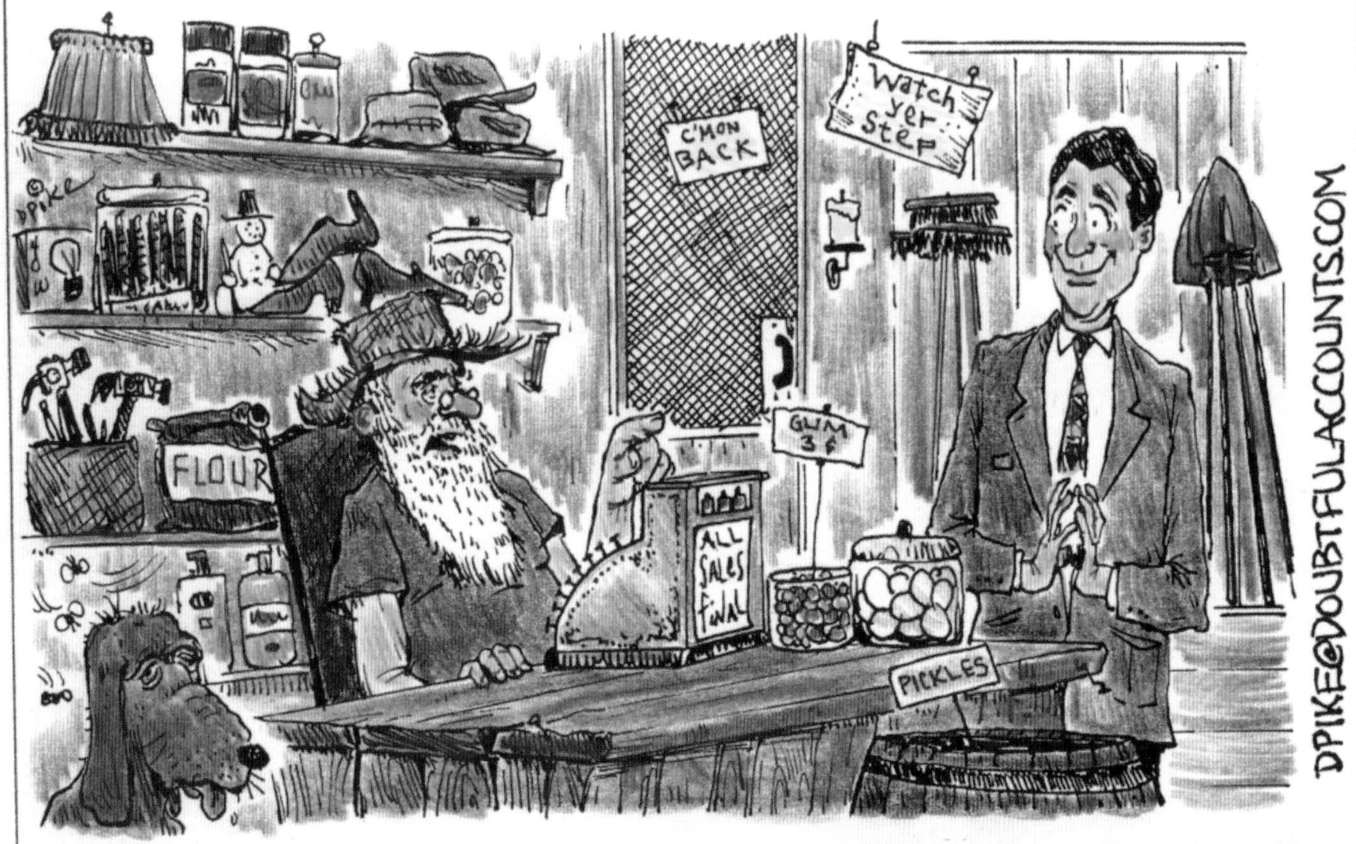
C'MON BACK
Watch yer step
FLOUR
ALL SALES FINAL
GUM 3¢
PICKLES
DPIKE@DOUBTFULACCOUNTS.COM

No, no white wine, just a couple cases of '64 Chateau Beychevelle back there between the beans and diapers—five bucks each.

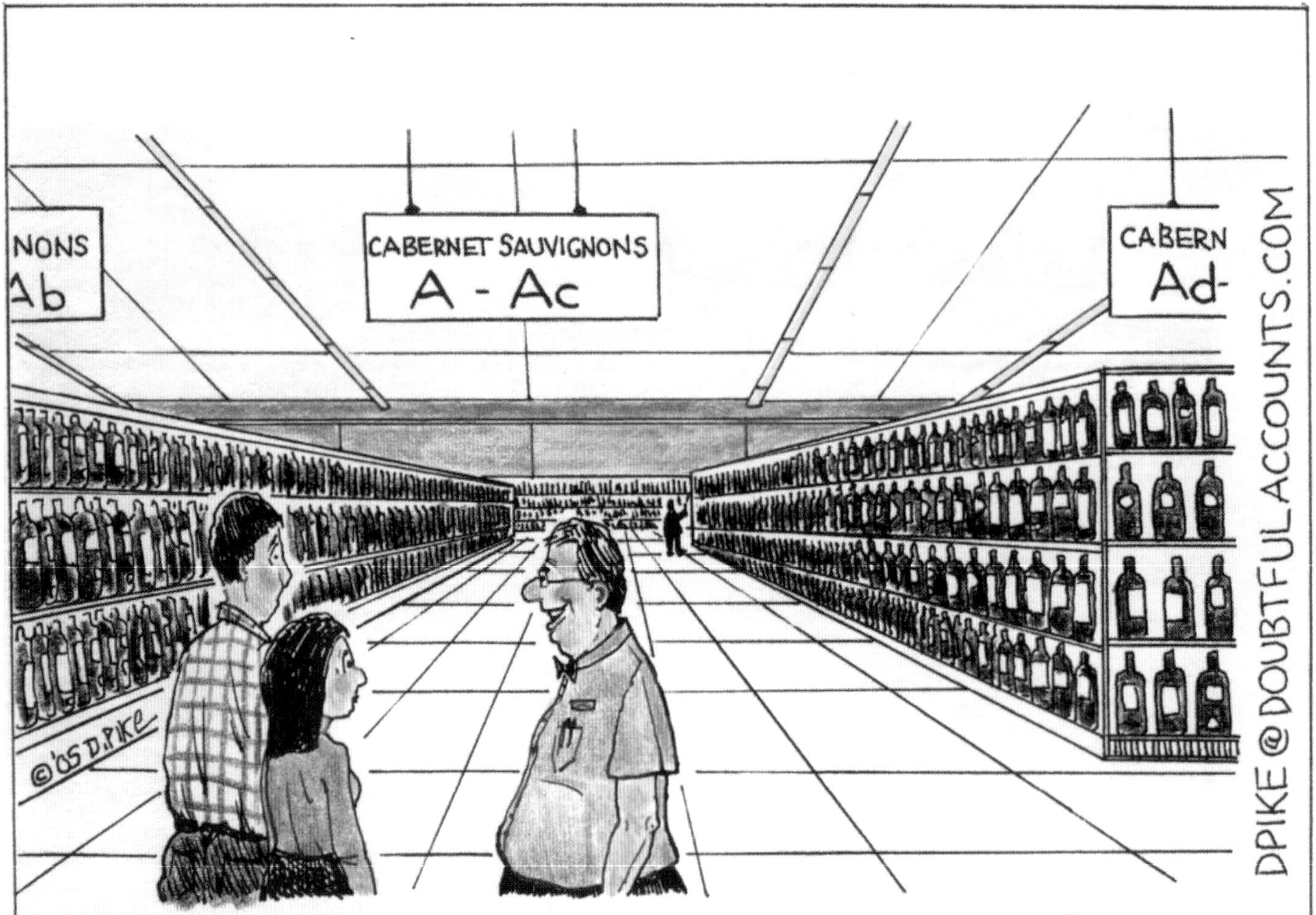
NONS
Ab
CABERNET SAUVIGNONS
A - Ac
CABERN
Ad-
©'05 D.PIKE
DPIKE @ DOUBTFULACCOUNTS.COM

If you're having trouble finding what you want, try our other store— "Cabernet Sauvignons Starting With the Letter B".

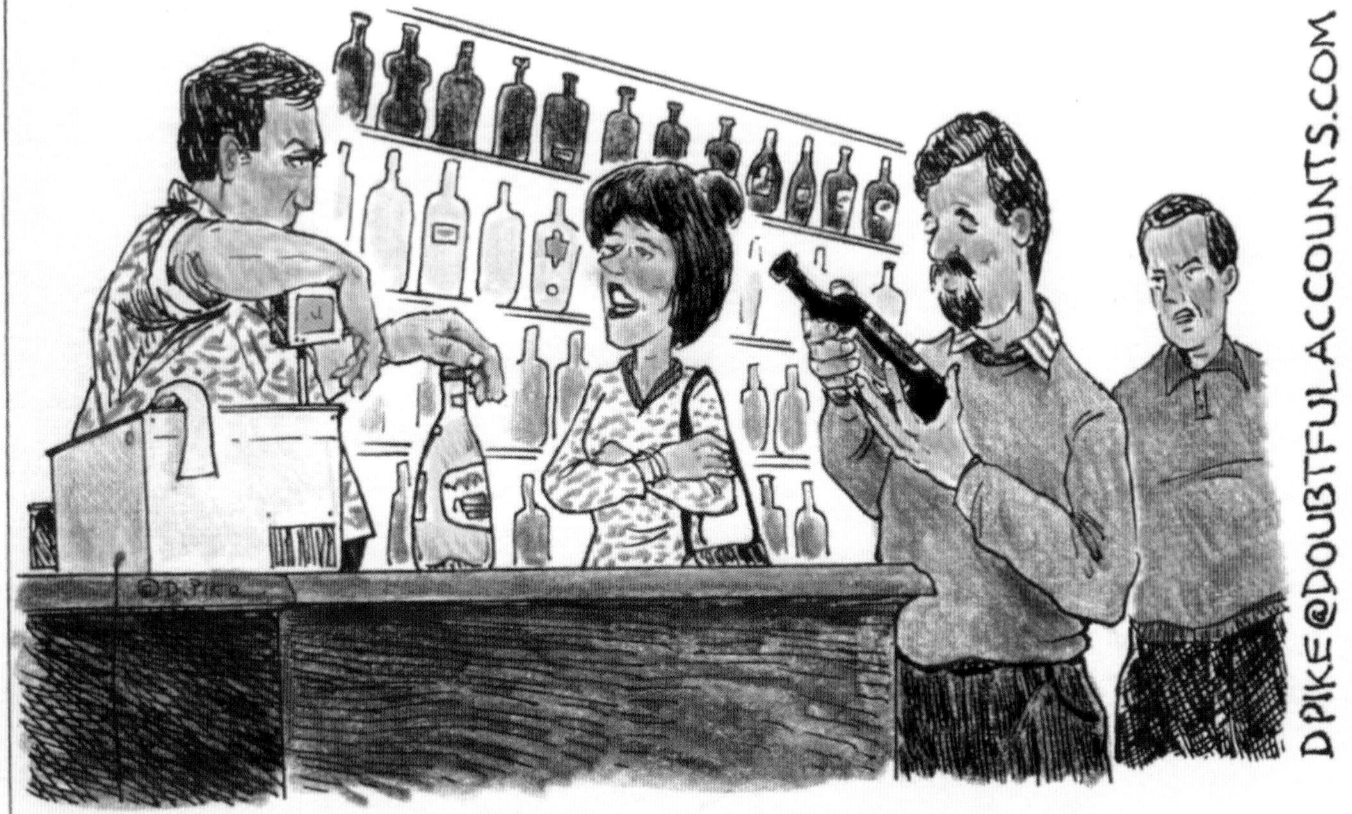
DPIKE@DOUBTFULACCOUNTS.COM

Toyota turns iron ore into pick-up trucks faster than my husband selects wine.

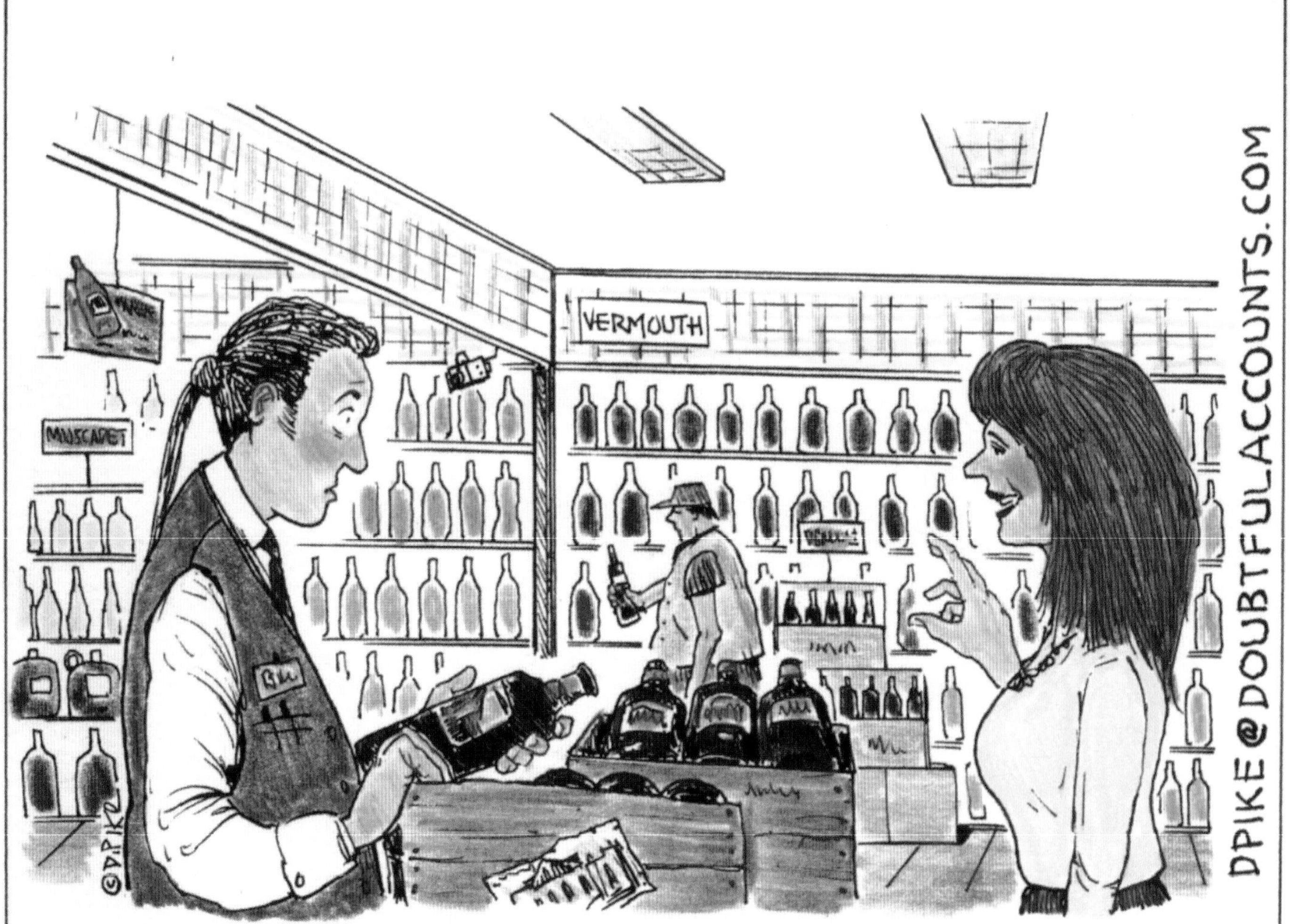
VERMOUTH
MUSCADET
©D.PIKE
DPIKE@DOUBTFULACCOUNTS.COM

Can you recommend a wine that will go well with the Burkes?

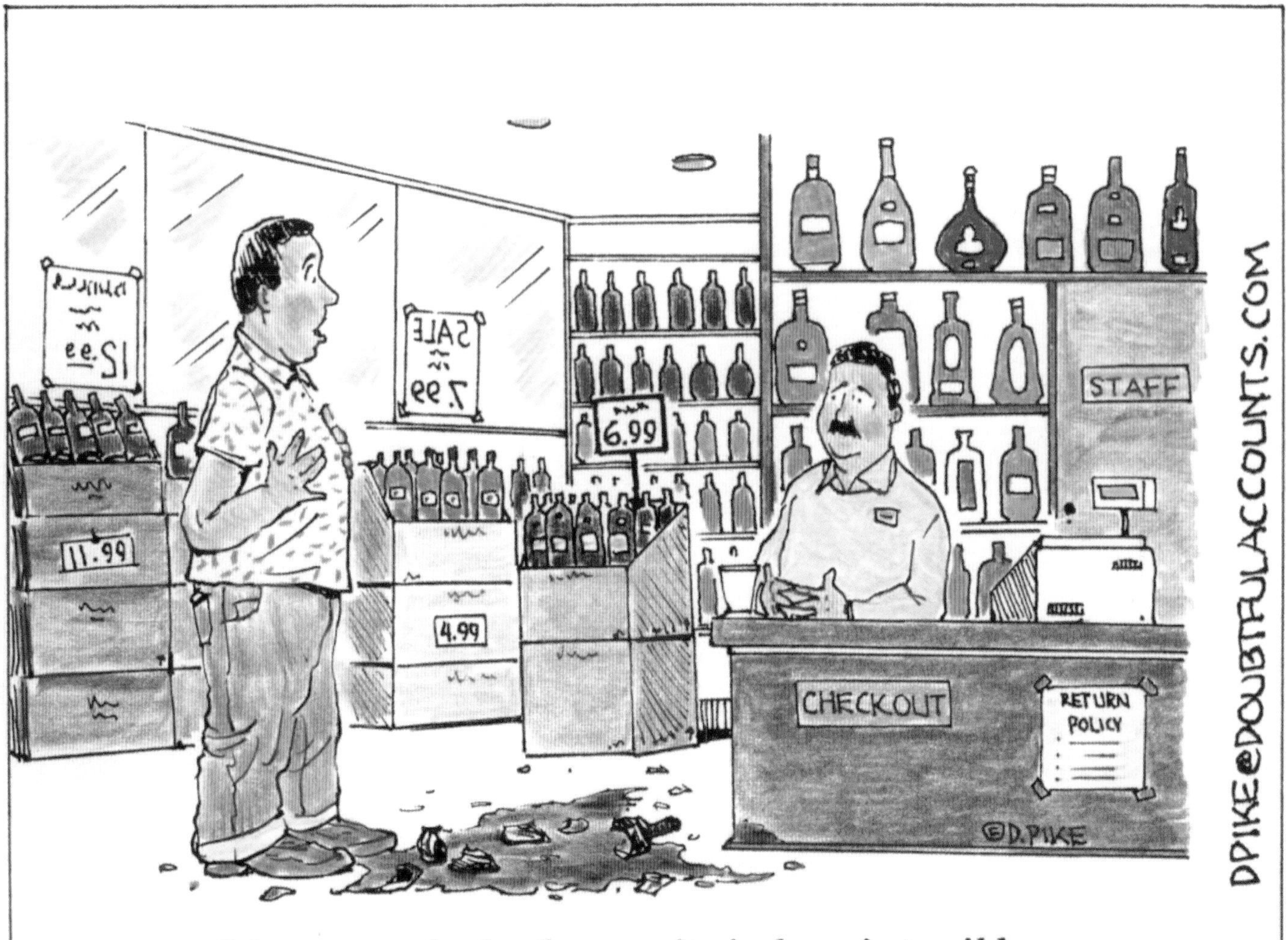
SALE
7.99
12.99
6.99
11.99
4.99
STAFF
CHECKOUT
RETURN POLICY
©D.PIKE
DPIKE@DOUBTFULACCOUNTS.COM

It's not my fault; the gravity in here is terrible.

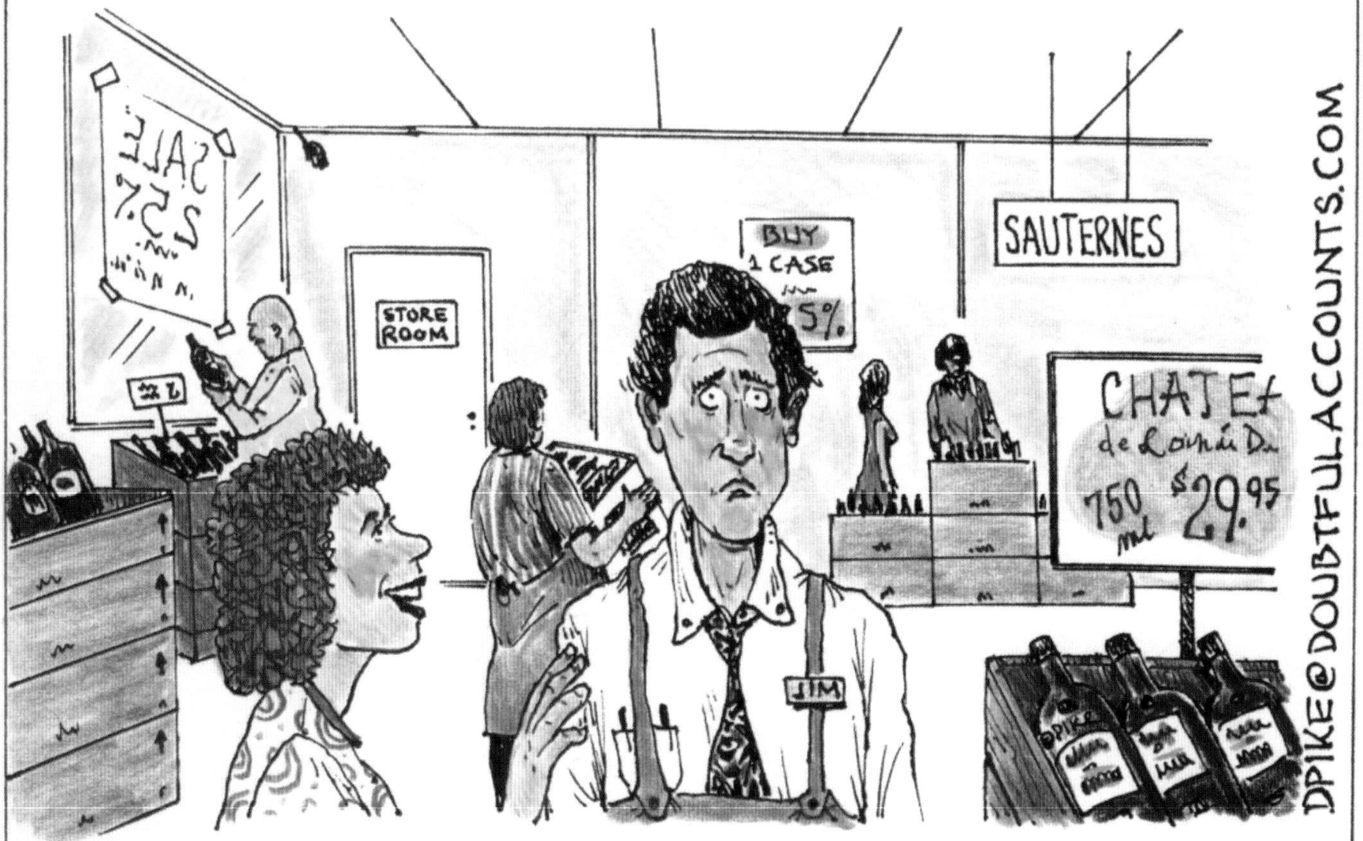
STORE ROOM
BUY 1 CASE 5%
SAUTERNES
750 ml $29.95
JIM
DPIKE@DOUBTFULACCOUNTS.COM

What have you got in the way of a Cabernet Sauvignon for people who like Zinfandel when they can't find Merlot?

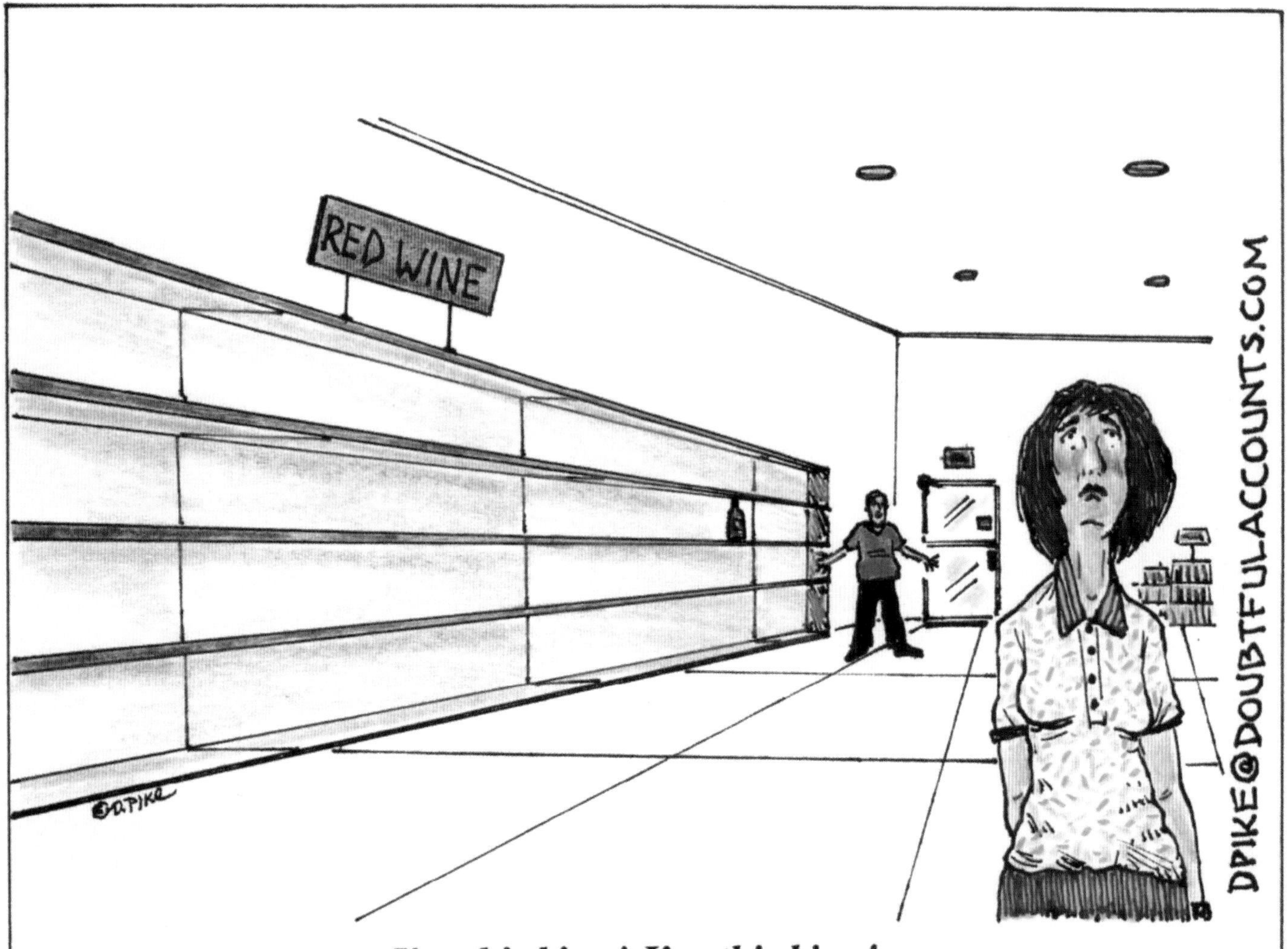
RED WINE
DPIKE@DOUBTFULACCOUNTS.COM

I'm thinking! I'm thinking!

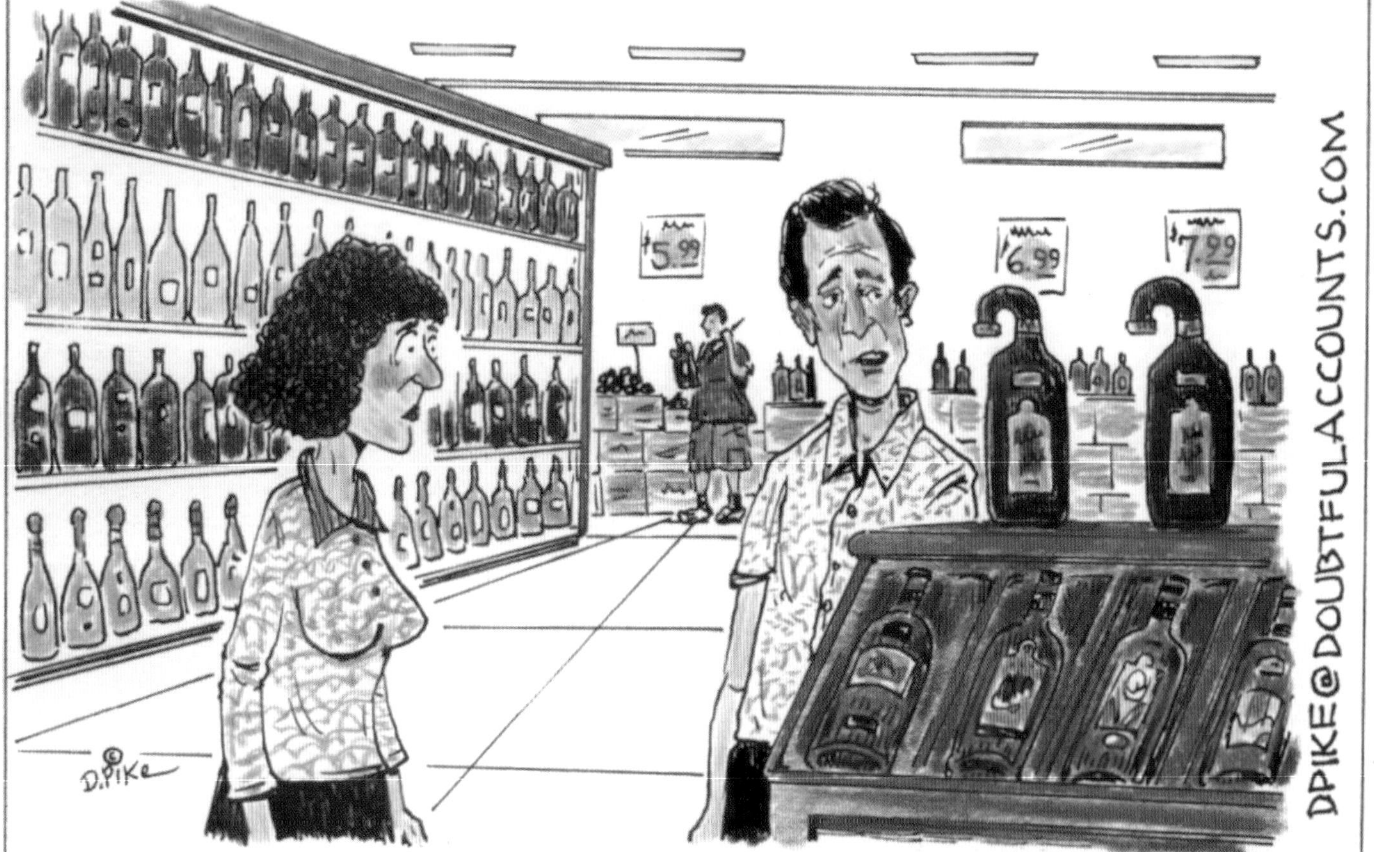
$5.99
$6.99
$7.99
D.PIKE ©
DPIKE@DOUBTFULACCOUNTS.COM

You wanted a soft wine? Look no further.

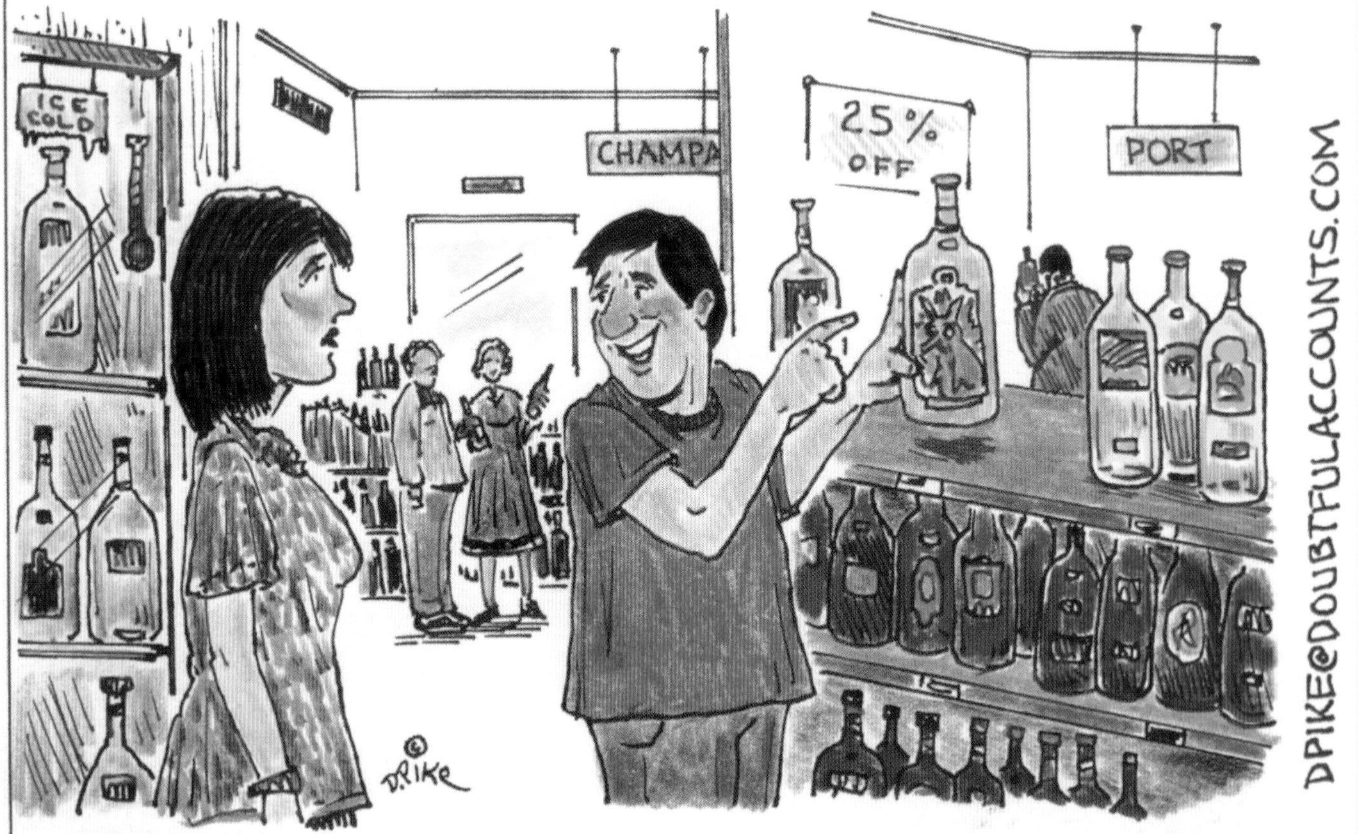
ICE COLD
CHAMPA
25% OFF
PORT
©
D.PIKE
DPIKE@DOUBTFULACCOUNTS.COM

Wow! Look at that one! It's got a flaming aardvark on the label! That's got to be good!

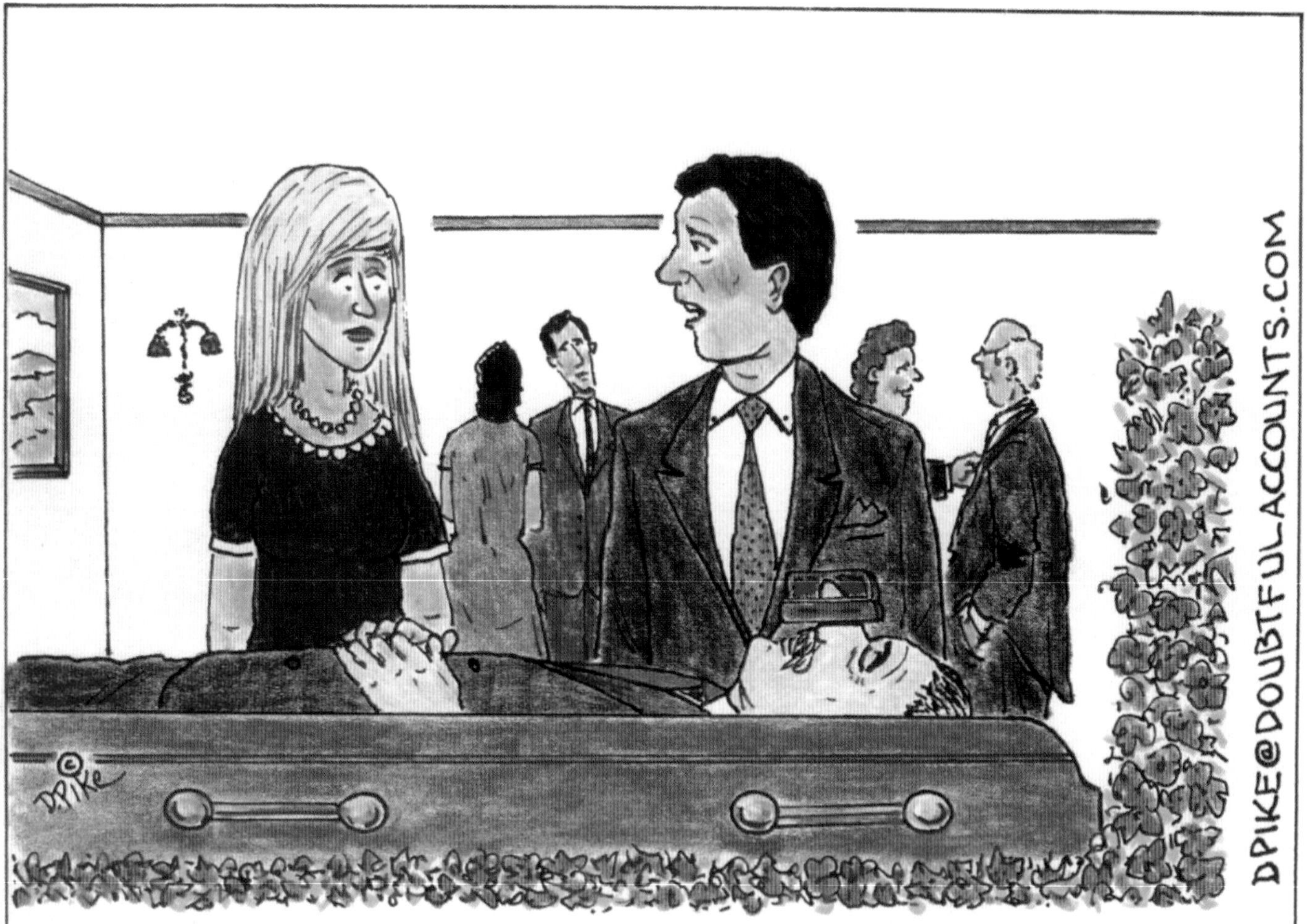

© D.PIKE
DPIKE@DOUBTFULACCOUNTS.COM

He was our head wine buyer for over 30 years, so it only seemed fitting.

2

Silence of the Lambruscos: The Uneasy Consumer

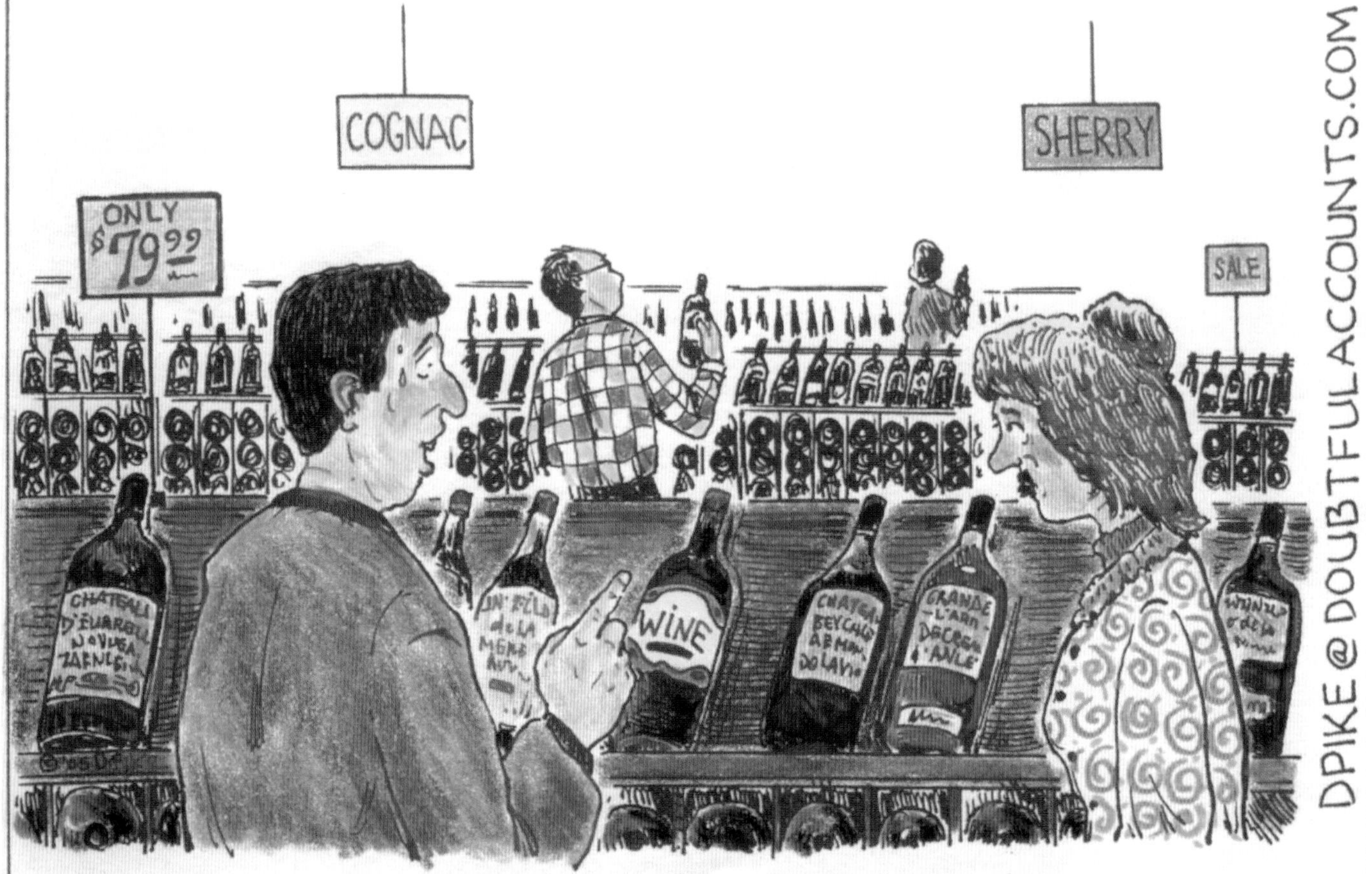
COGNAC
SHERRY
ONLY $79.99
SALE
WINE
DPIKE@DOUBTFULACCOUNTS.COM

Honey, this one sounds good.

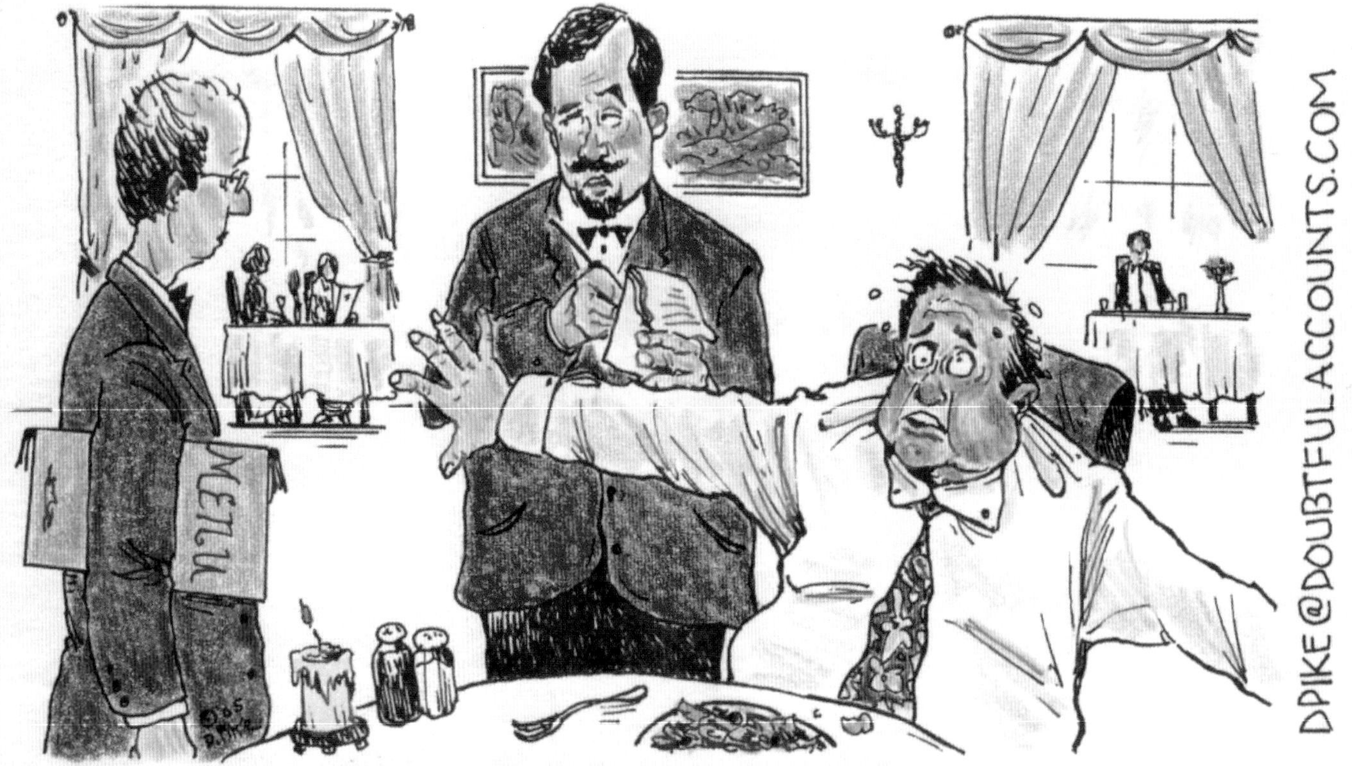
MENU
DPIKE@DOUBTFULACCOUNTS.COM

You think he's gagging on a crouton, too?
I think he's just trying to say Gewurztraminer.

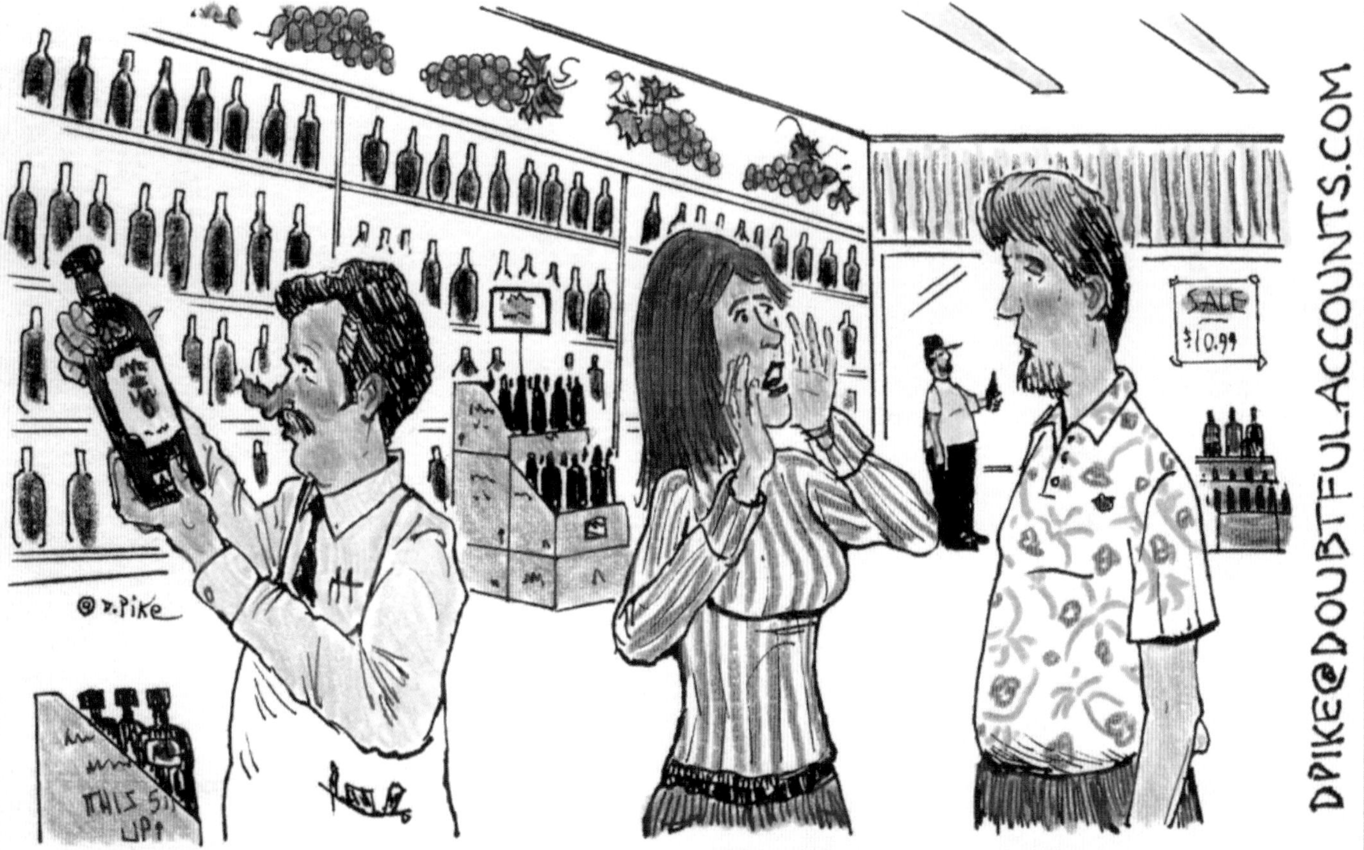
SALE
$10.99
© D.Pike
DPIKE@DOUBTFULACCOUNTS.COM

How do we ask for a first growth Bordeaux without using the word growth?

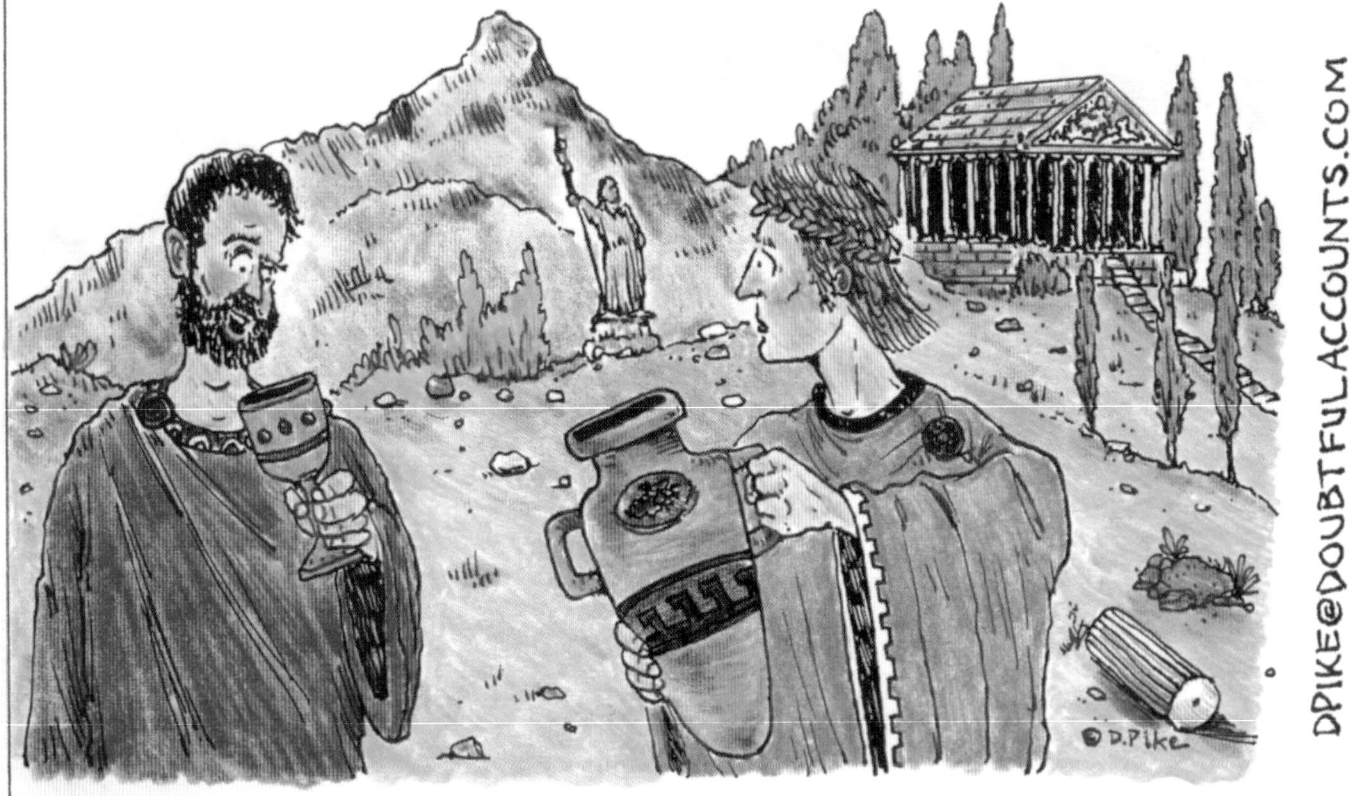
© D.Pike
DPIKE@DOUBTFULACCOUNTS.COM

You paid three goats for this? Robertus Parkerus only rated it LXXIV.

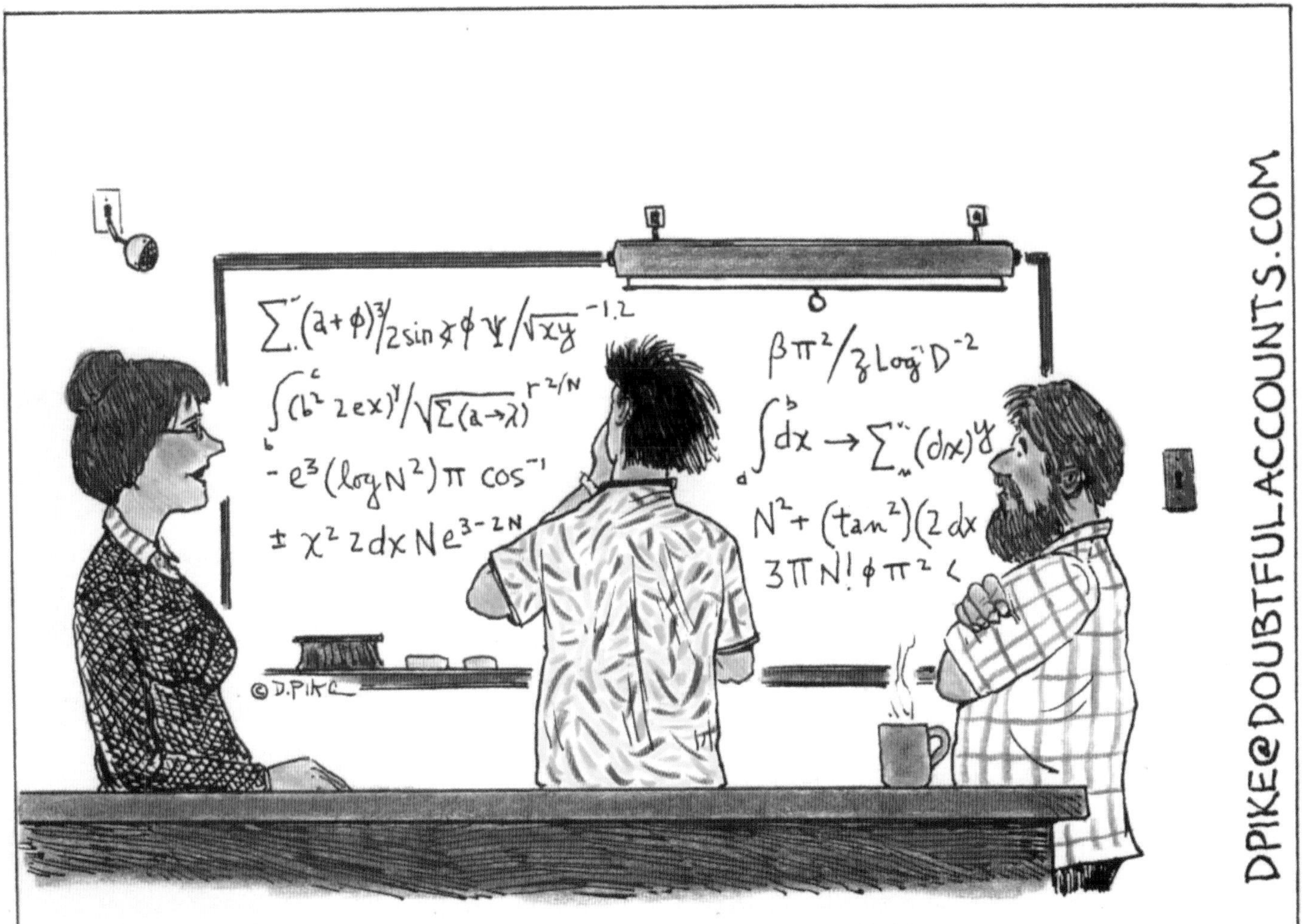
© D.PIKE
DPIKE@DOUBTFULACCOUNTS.COM

I know he'll solve it—he even understands German wine labels.

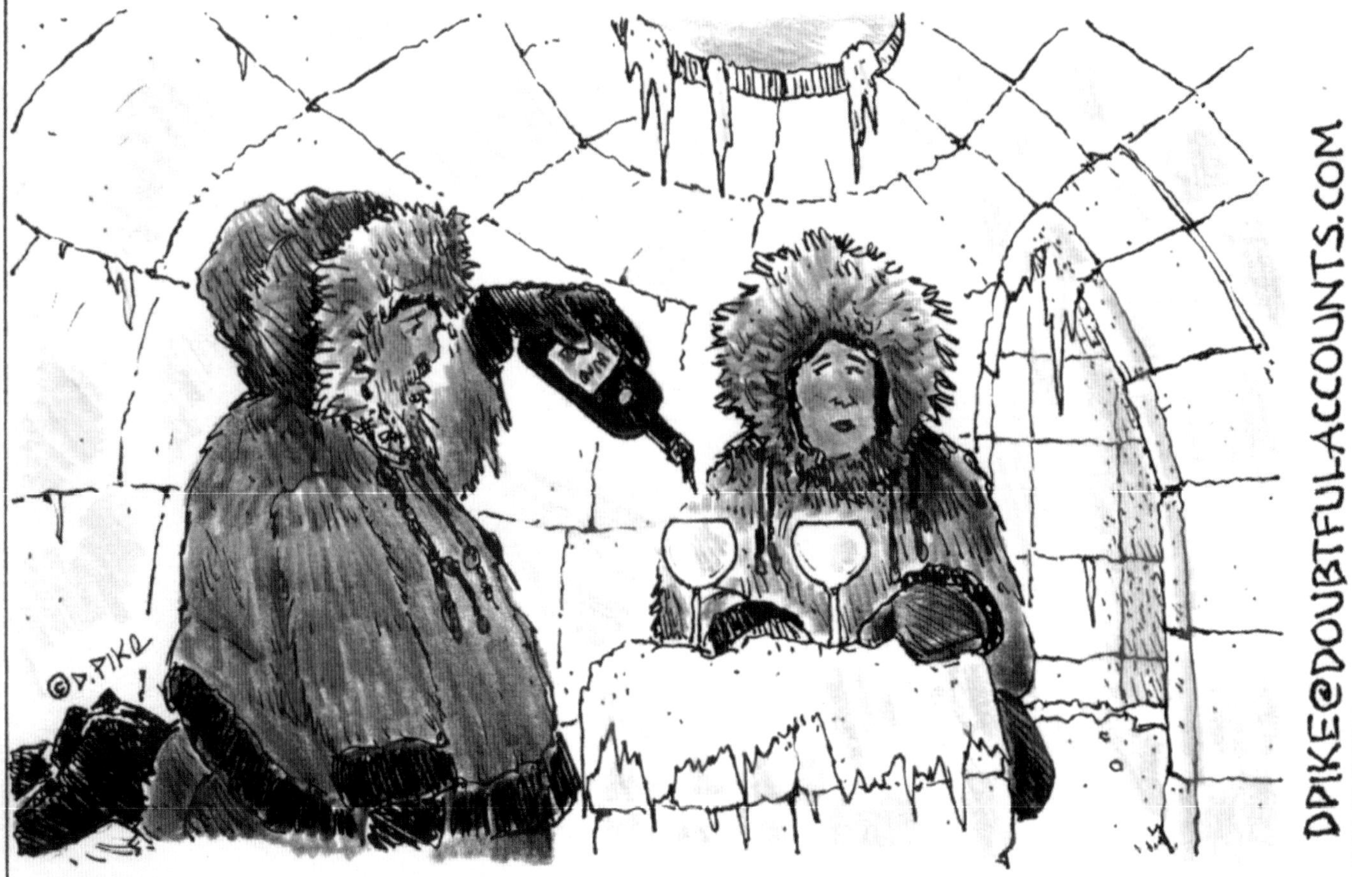
©D.PIKE
DPIKE@DOUBTFULACCOUNTS.COM

I don't get it. They told me to serve merlot at room temperature.

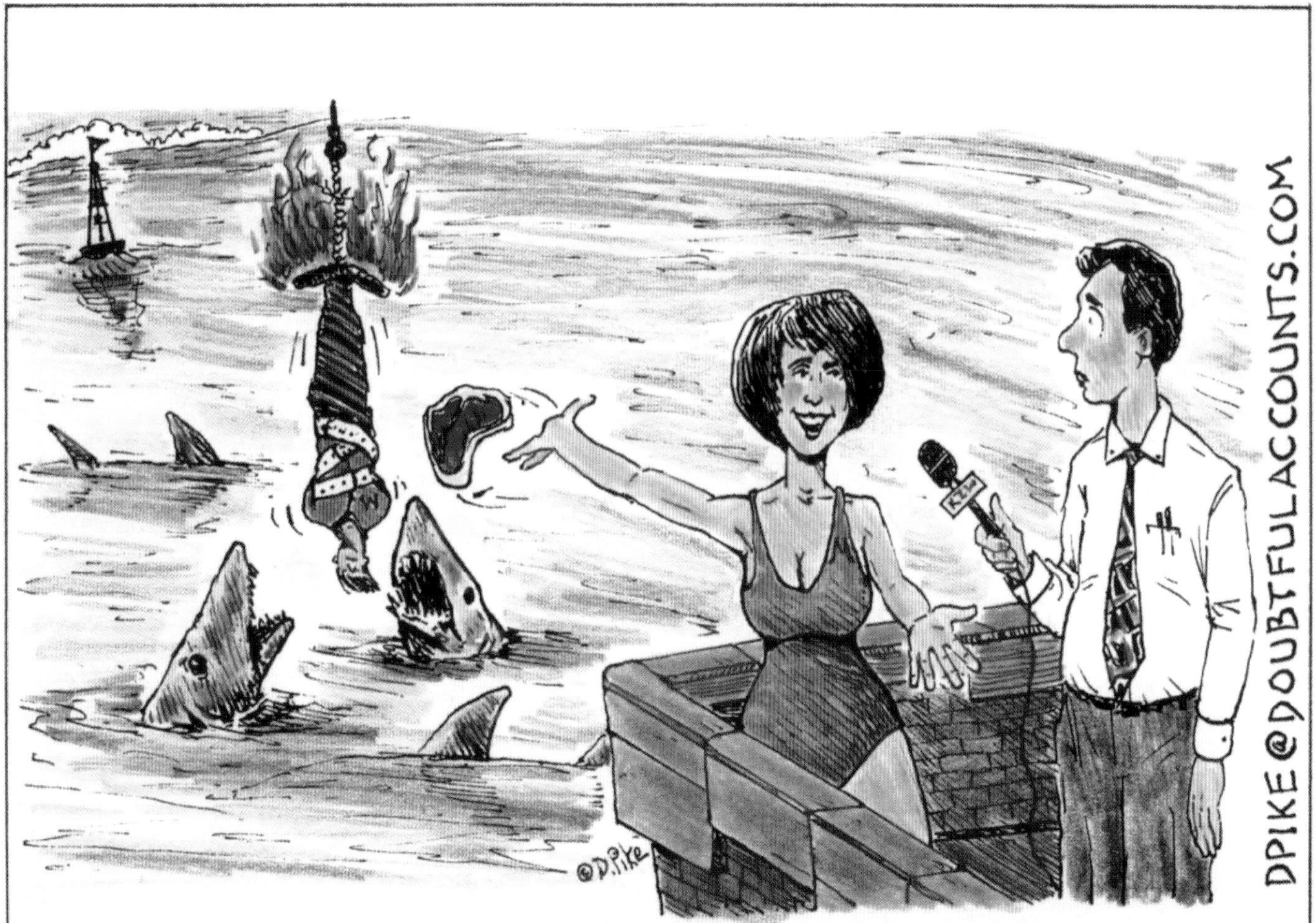
DPIKE@DOUBTFULACCOUNTS.COM
©D.Pike

Dangerous? You should have been there when he ordered a bottle of New York State Champagne in Paris—<u>that</u> was dangerous!

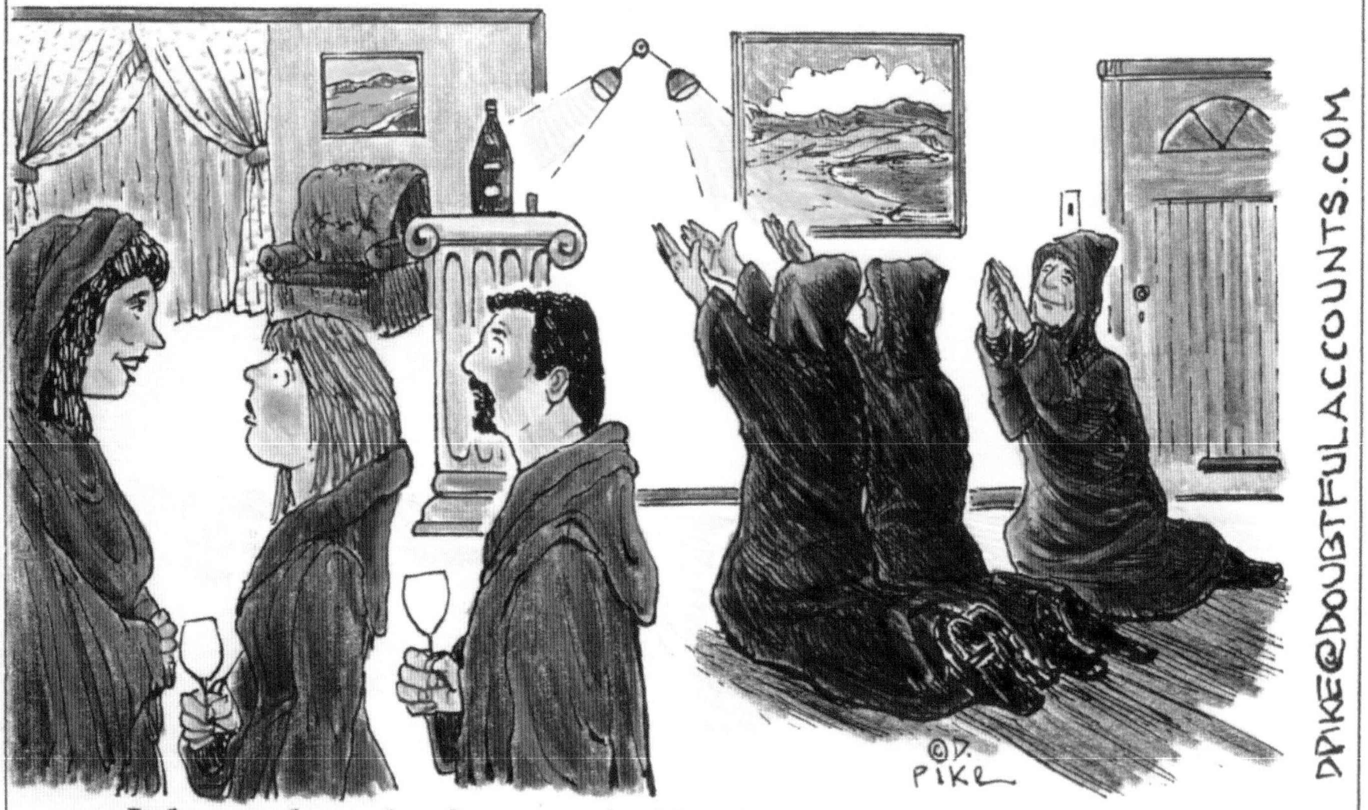
©D. PIKE
DPIKE@DOUBTFULACCOUNTS.COM

It has to breathe for exactly 22 minutes; then I can pour you a glass—right after the sacrifice.

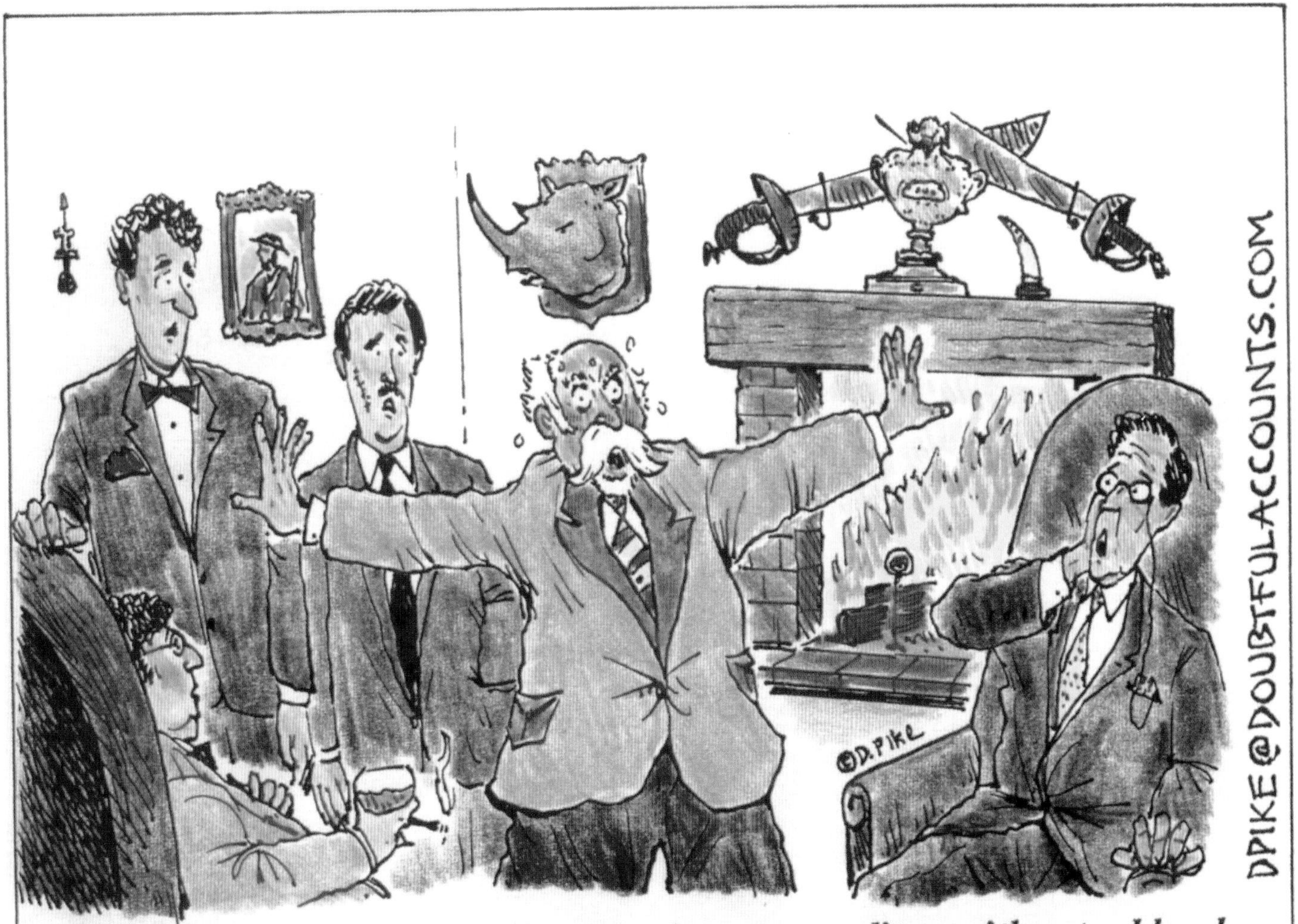
©D.PIKE
DPIKE@DOUBTFULACCOUNTS.COM

So there I was, alone in the aisle, heart pounding, without a bloody clue as to what wine I should bring our hosts.

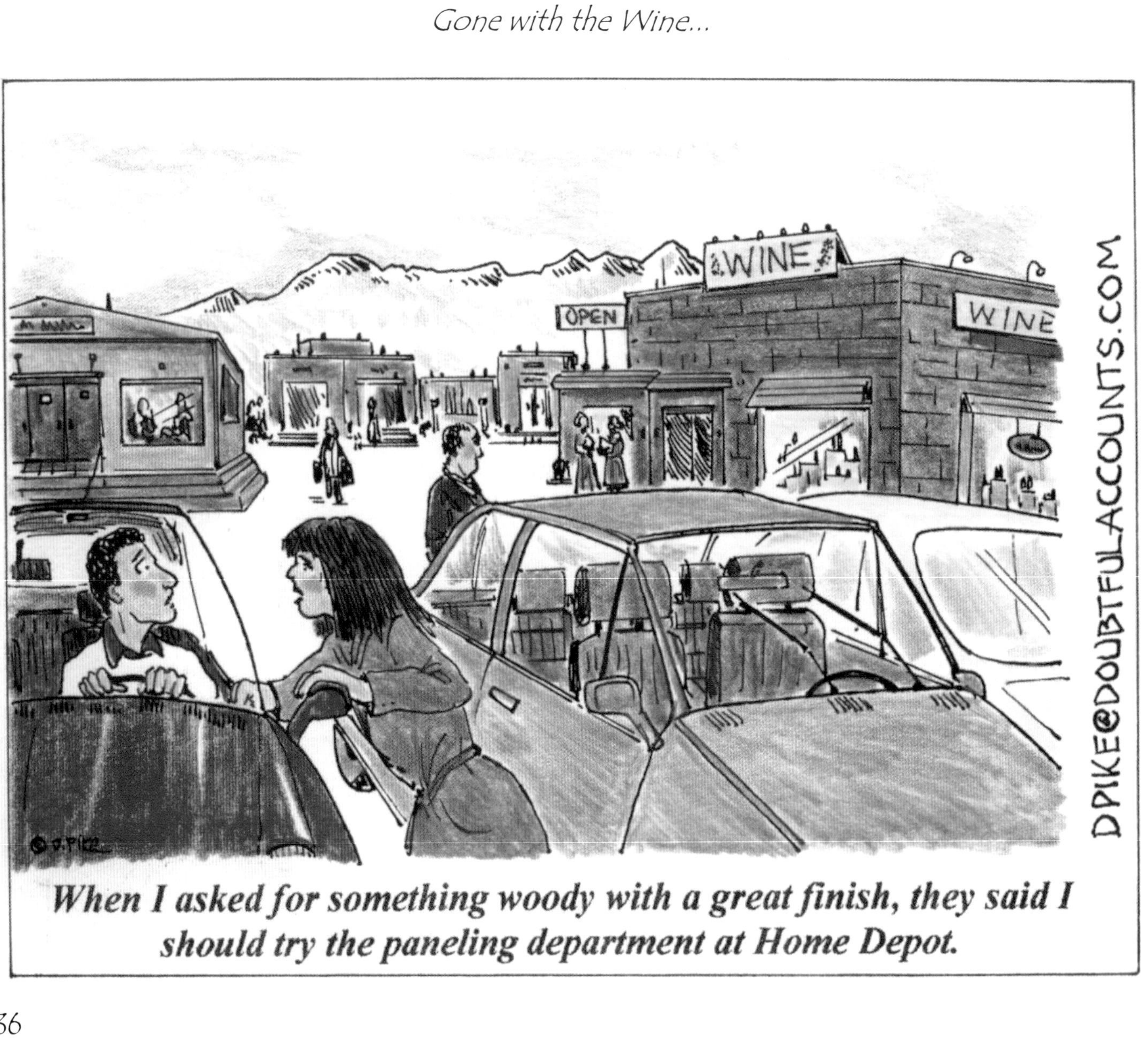
WINE
OPEN
WINE
© D.PIKE
DPIKE@DOUBTFULACCOUNTS.COM

When I asked for something woody with a great finish, they said I should try the paneling department at Home Depot.

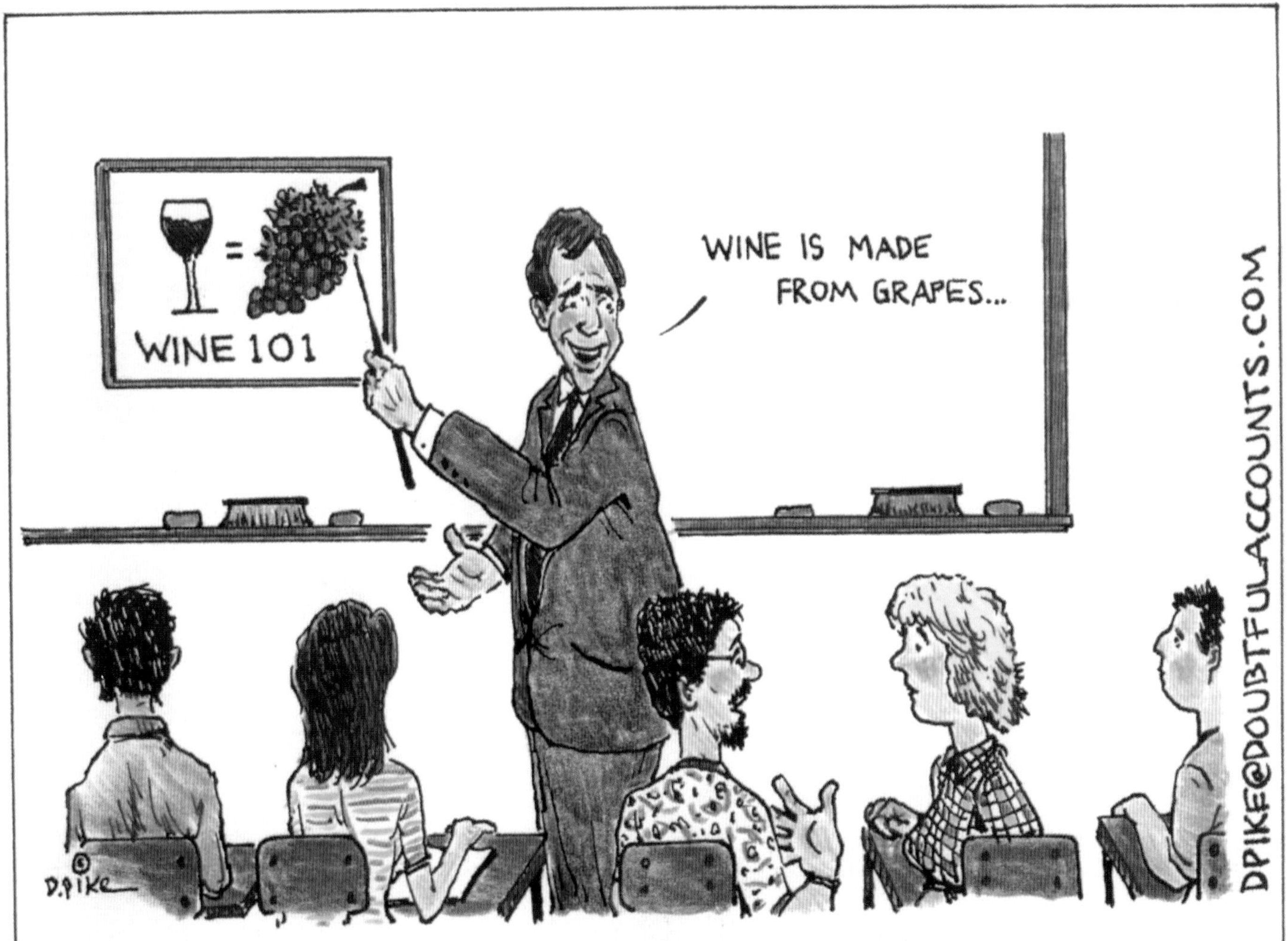
WINE 101
WINE IS MADE FROM GRAPES...
© D.PIKE
DPIKE@DOUBTFULACCOUNTS.COM

I don't get it. Ask him to start over.

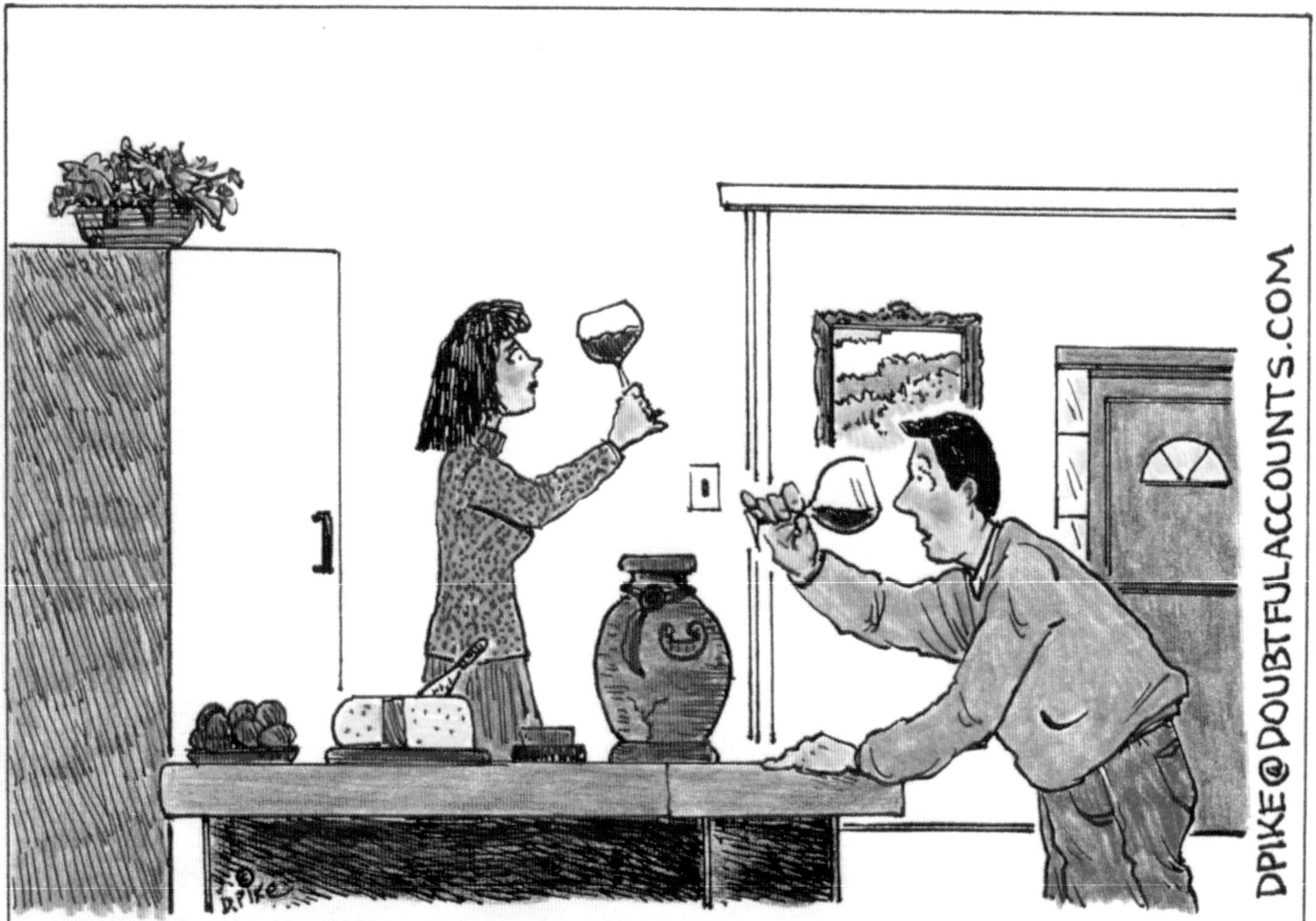
DPIKE@DOUBTFULACCOUNTS.COM
© D.PIKE

My luck, I buy a bottle of wine from 450 B.C. and it's still five years from reaching maturity.

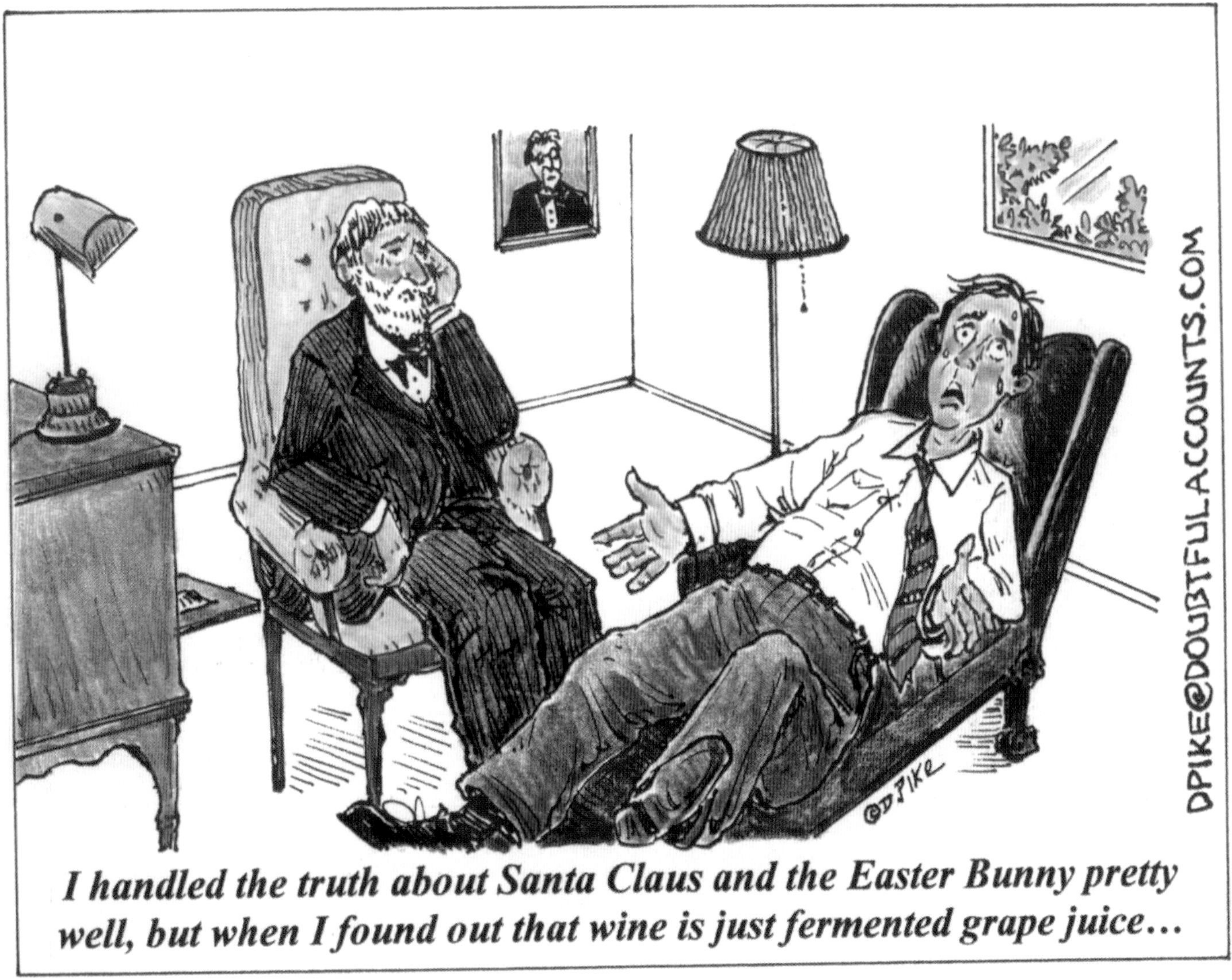
DPIKE@DOUBTFULACCOUNTS.COM
©D.PIKE

I handled the truth about Santa Claus and the Easter Bunny pretty well, but when I found out that wine is just fermented grape juice…

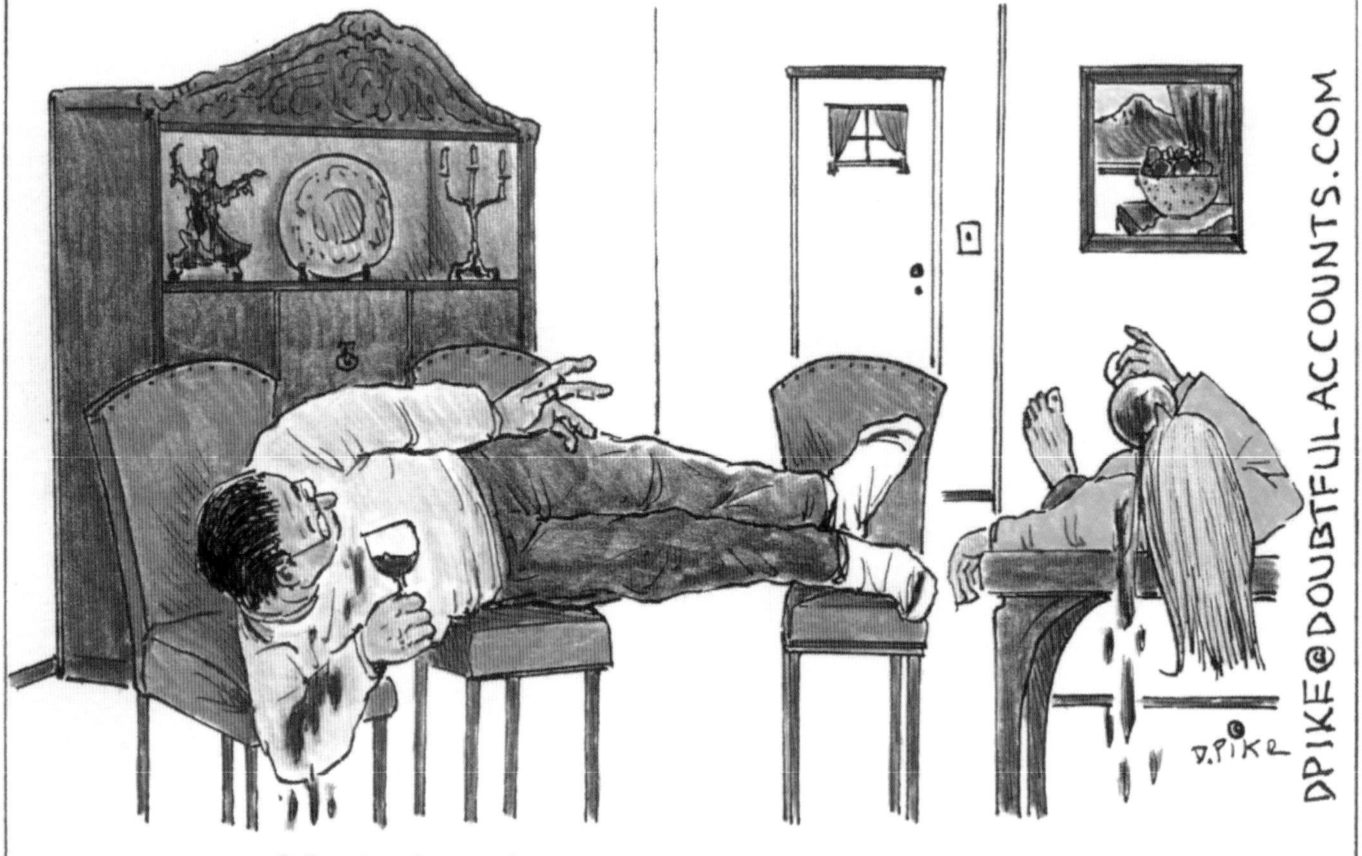
DPIKE@DOUBTFULACCOUNTS.COM
D.PIKE

Maybe he said store the wine horizontally…

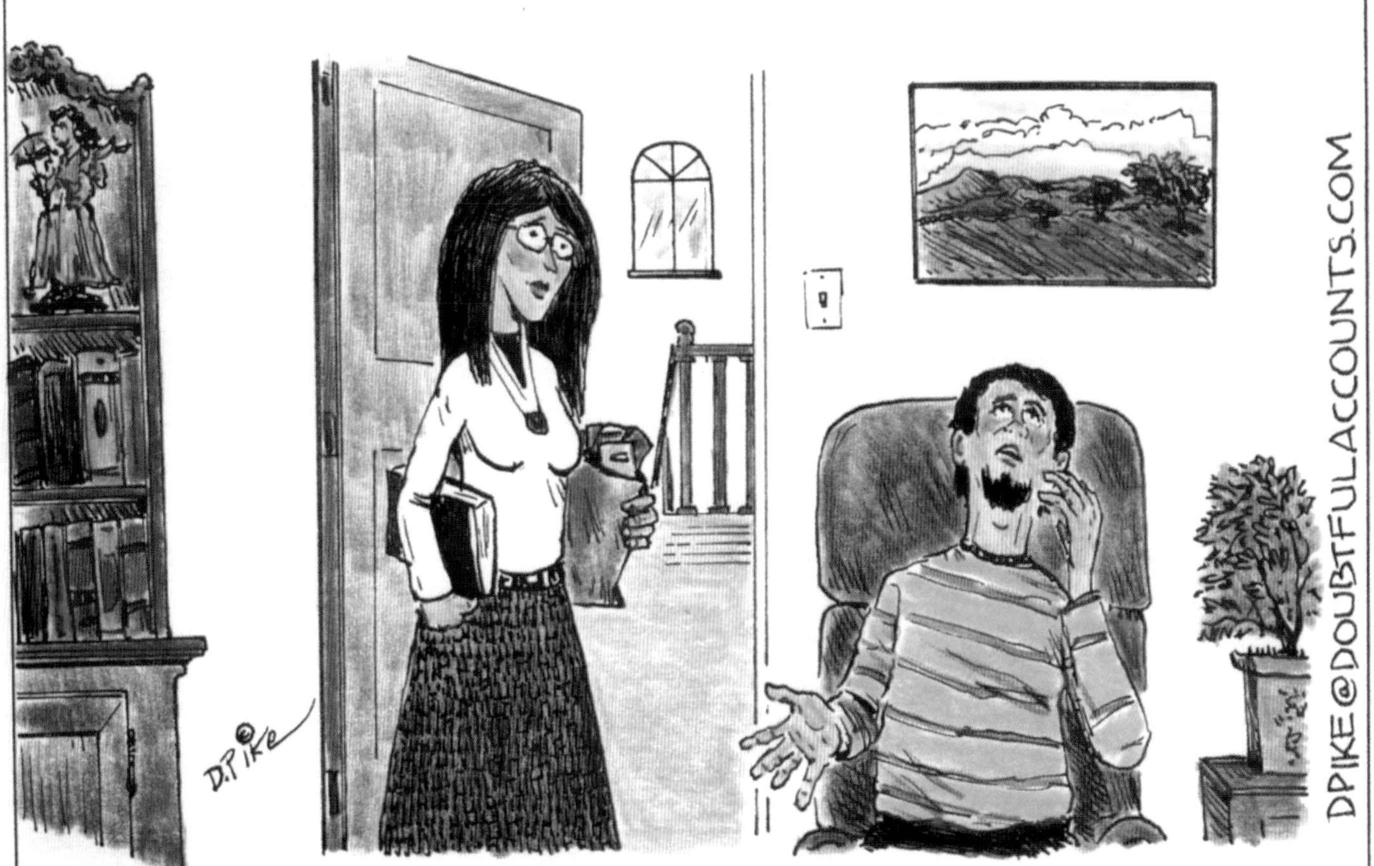
D.Pike
DPIKE@DOUBTFULACCOUNTS.COM

I failed my wine appreciation class. I swirled, sniffed and spilled out every sample perfectly. If only I had remembered to taste them.

3

Beauty and the Yeast:
The Waiter's Lament

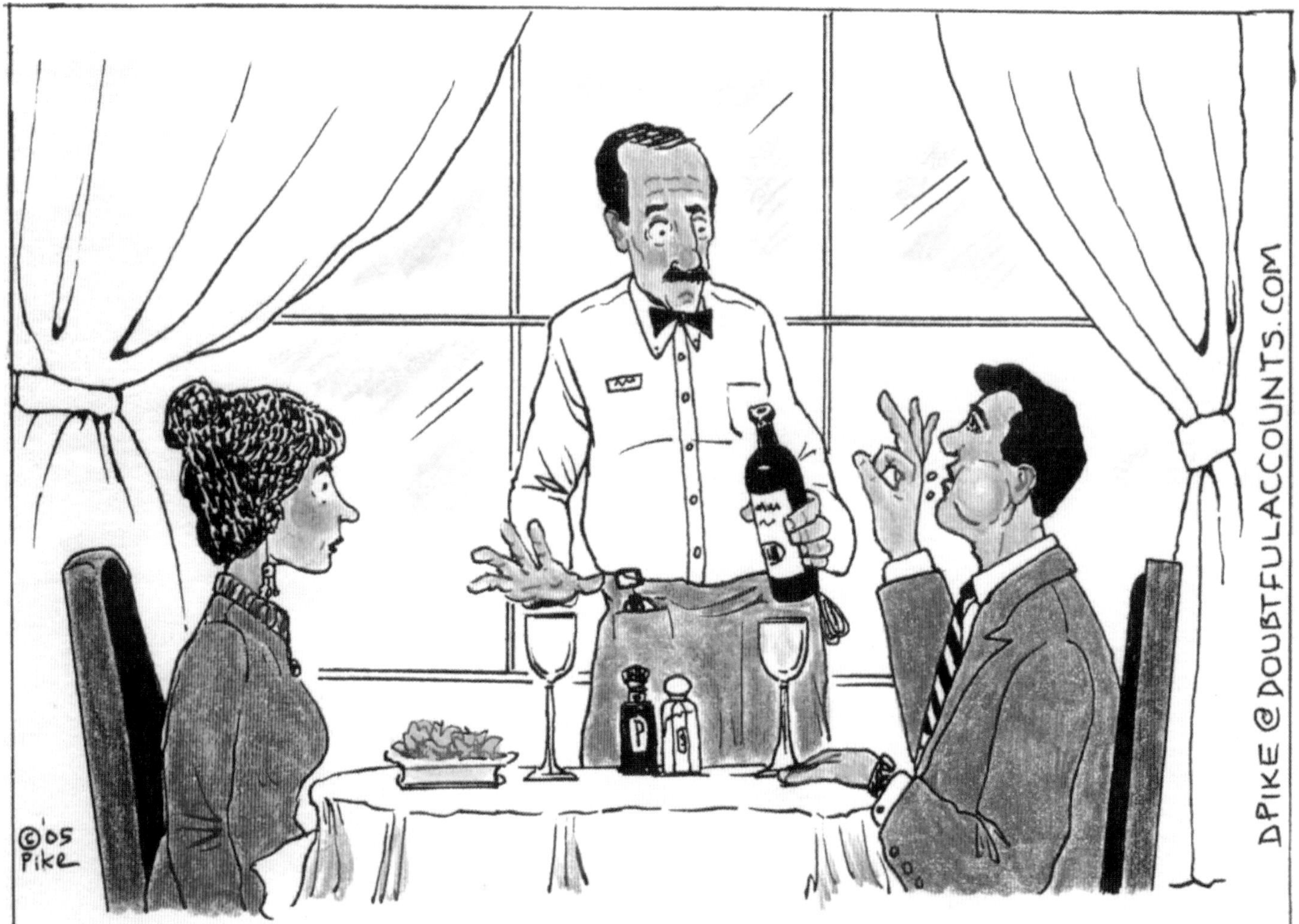
©'05
Pike
DPIKE@DOUBTFULACCOUNTS.COM

Excellent cork, go ahead and pour.

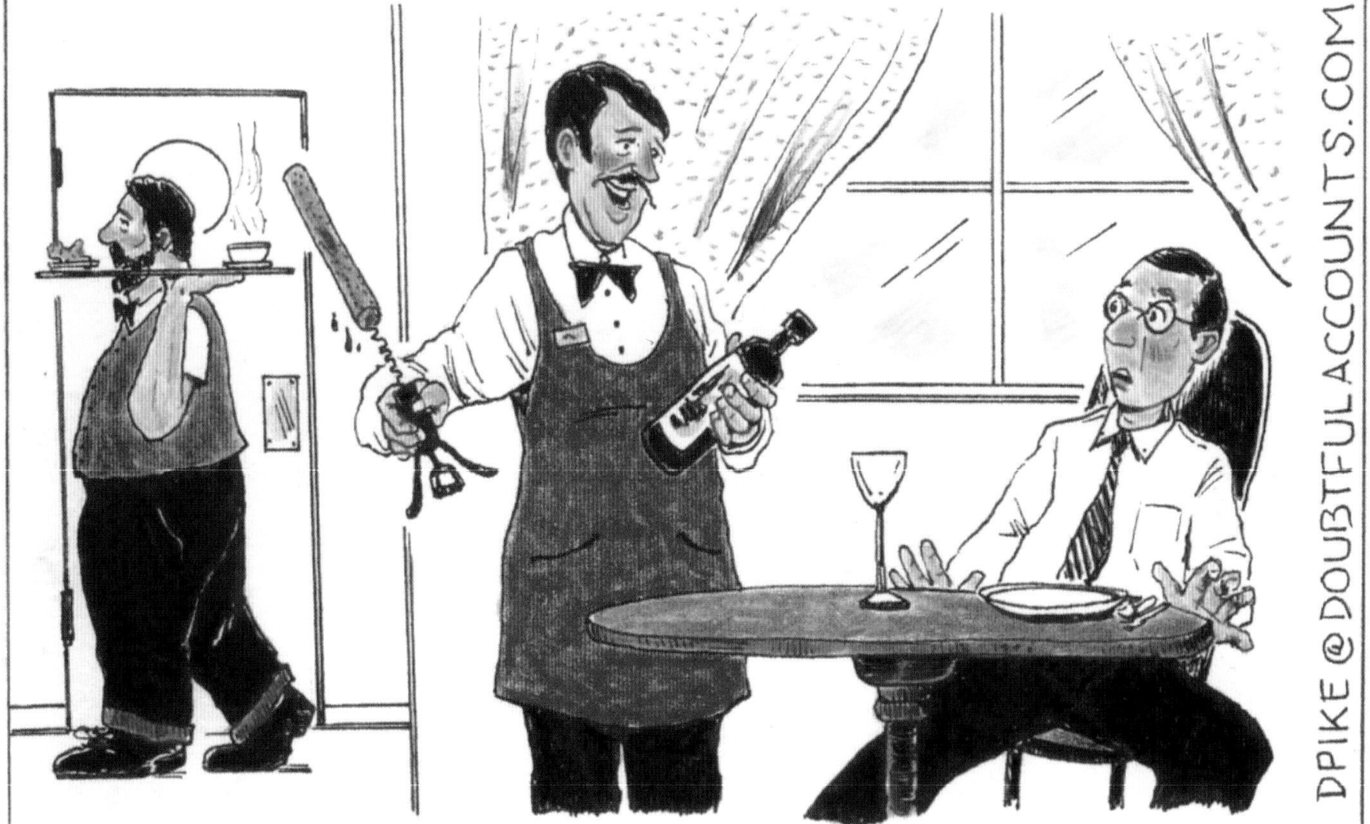
DPIKE @ DOUBTFULACCOUNTS.COM

Vino News only rates this wine a 2—but the cork got a 10!

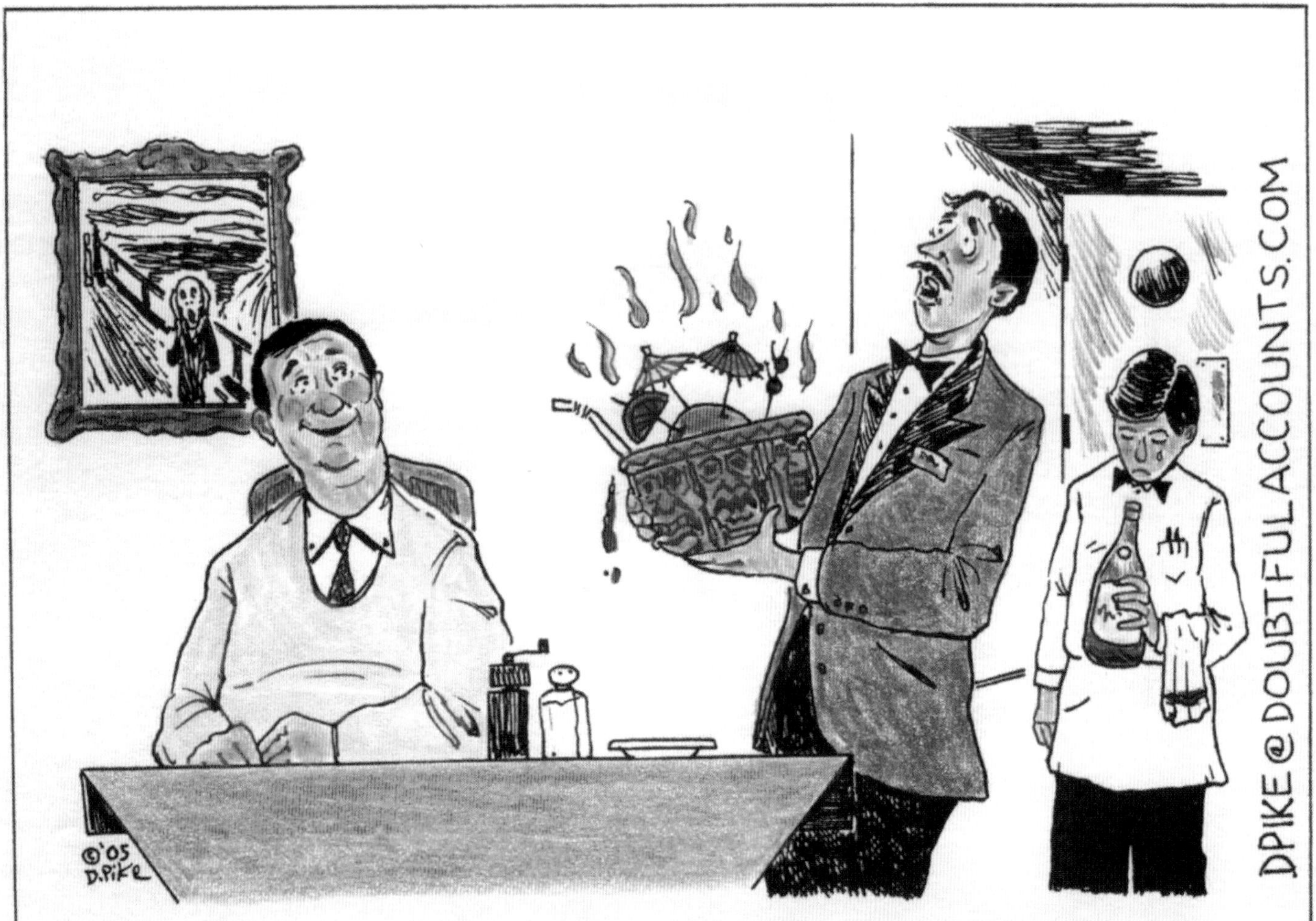
©'05
D.Pike
DPIKE@DOUBTFULACCOUNTS.COM

The '78 Gevrey-Chambertin, according to your directions, sir;
If you need me, I'll be in the storeroom, blowing my brains out.

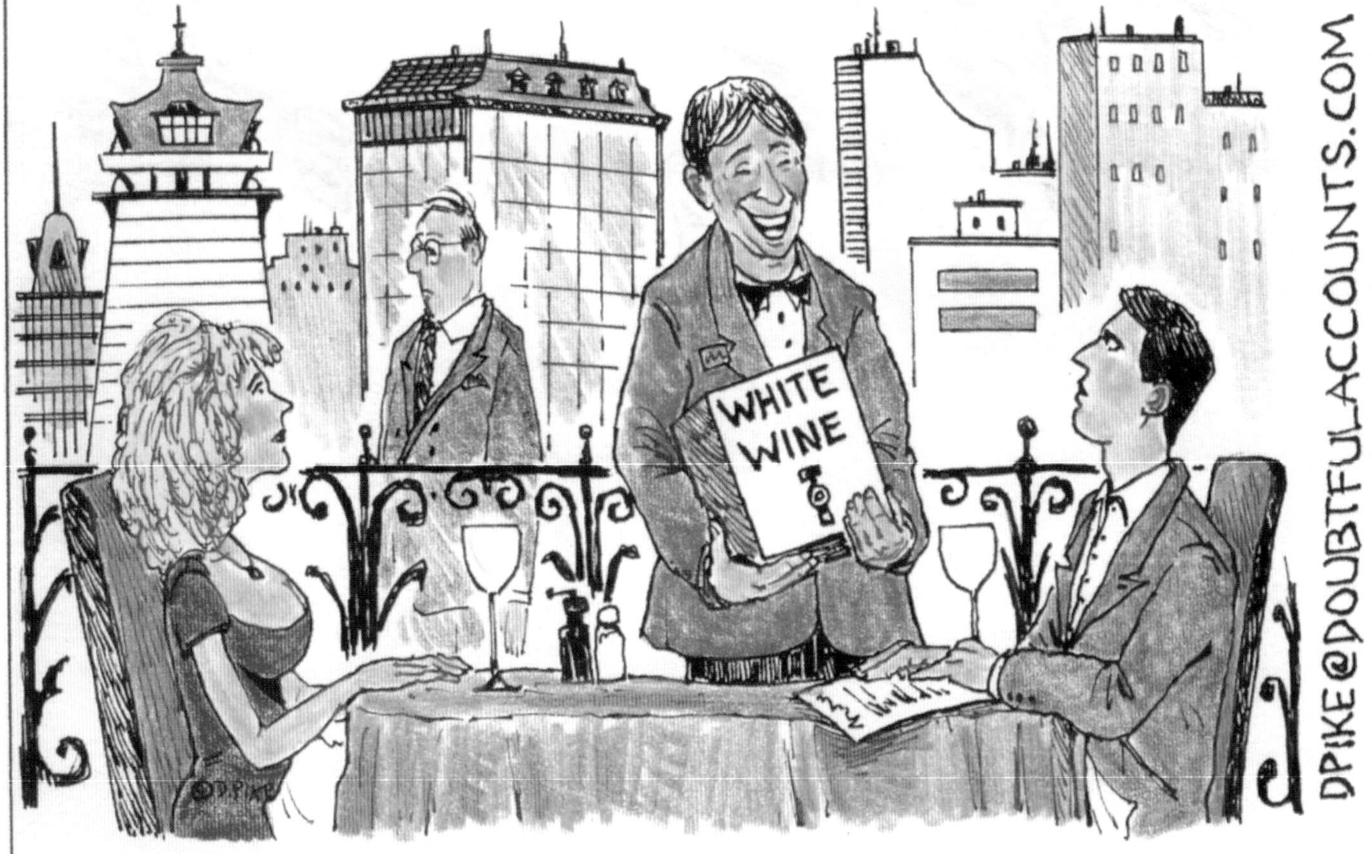
WHITE
WINE
DPIKE@DOUBTFULACCOUNTS.COM

"Excellent" choice, monsieur, would you care to sniff the spigot?

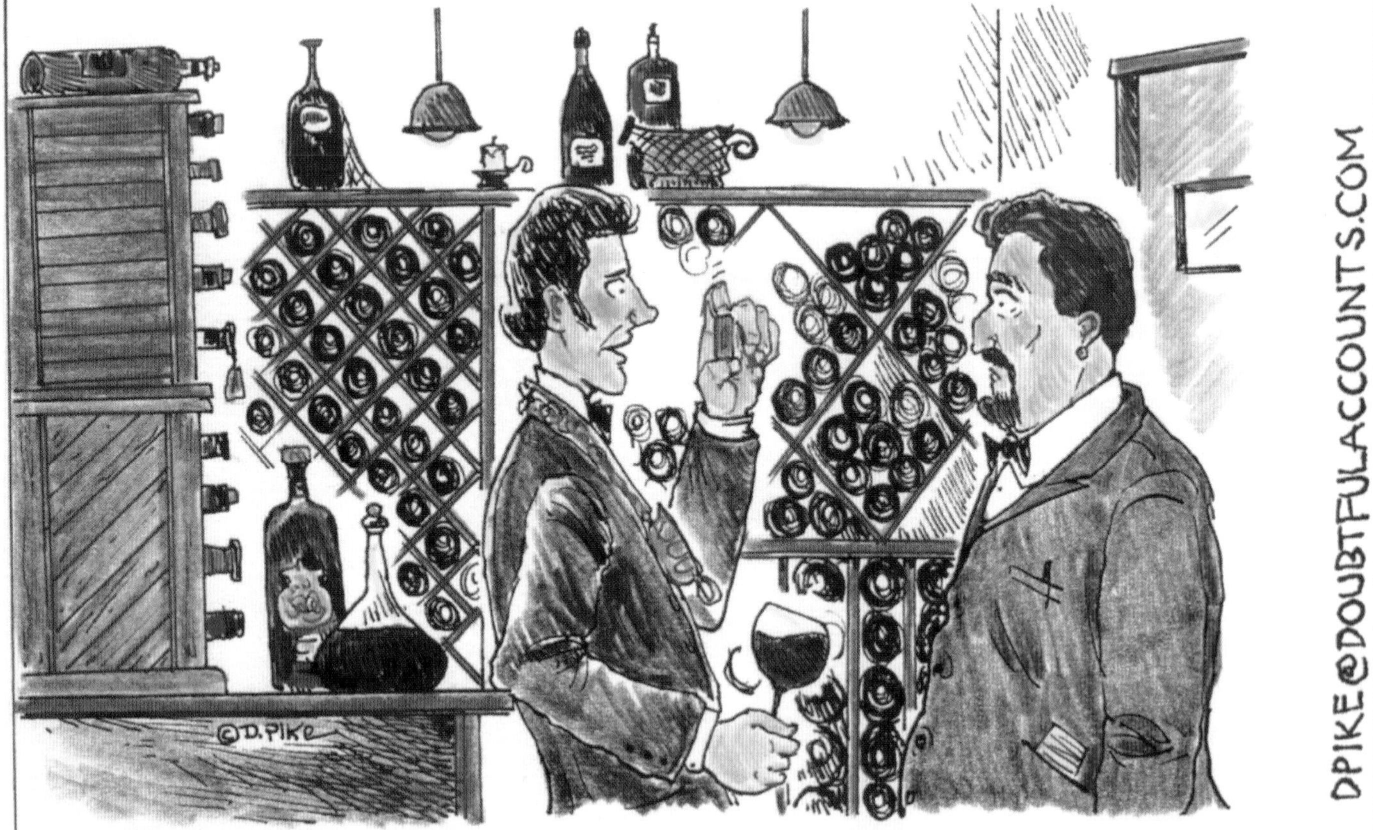
©D.PIKE
DPIKE@DOUBTFULACCOUNTS.COM

Plastic corks, then screw caps; when they come out with a flip-n-sip Chateau Petrus I'm hanging up my tastevin.

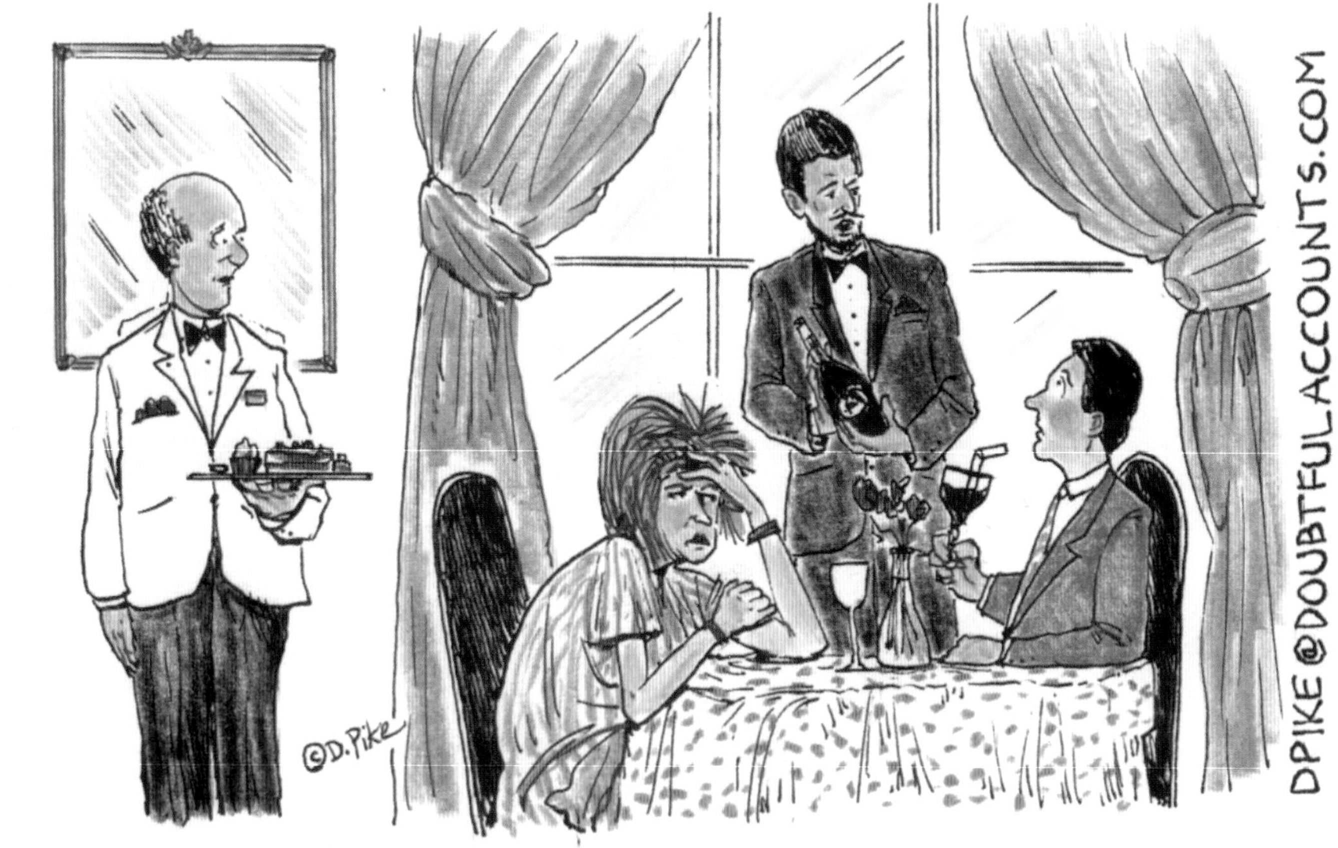
©D.Pike
DPIKE@DOUBTFULACCOUNTS.COM

No, I don't want to see you "make bubbles".

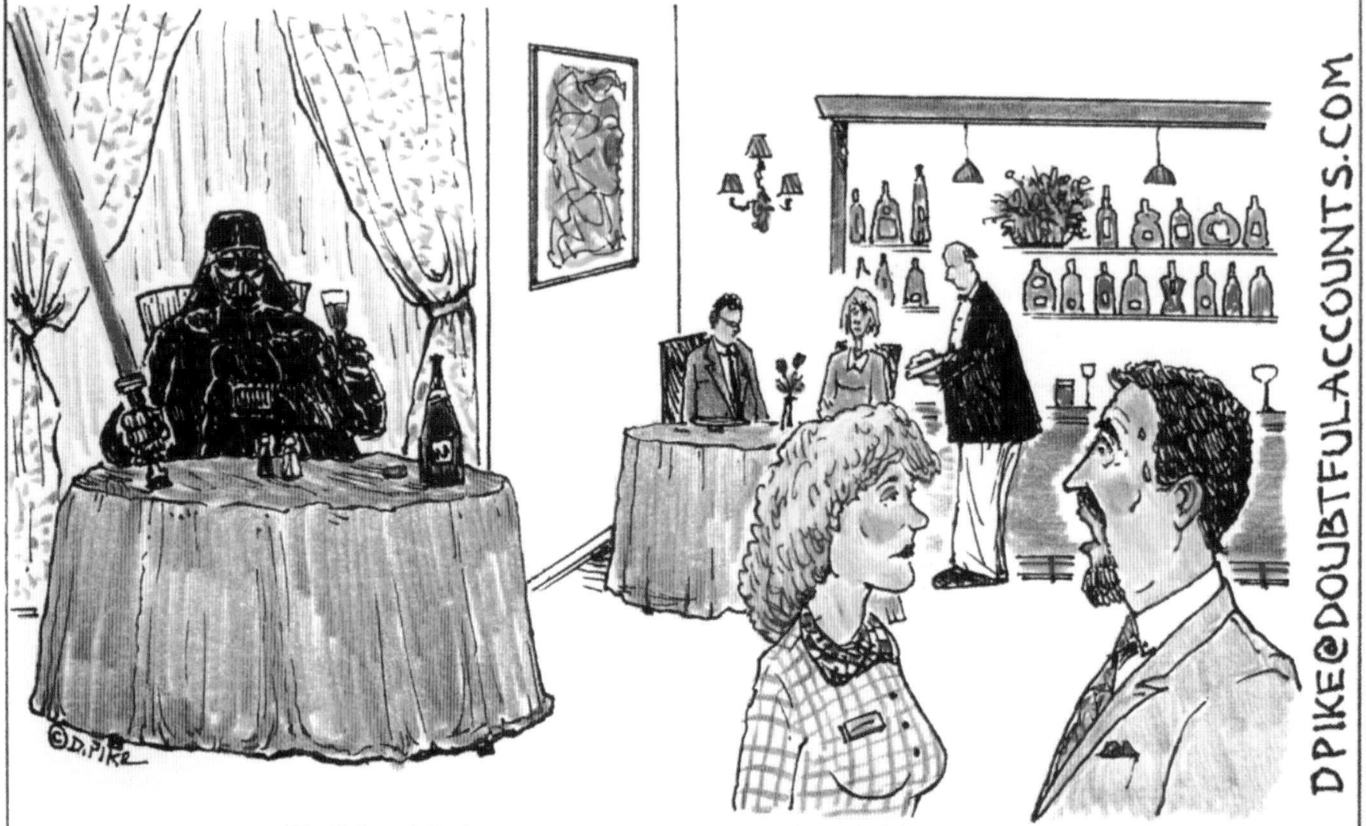
©D.PIKE
DPIKE@DOUBTFULACCOUNTS.COM

Table 12 has a complaint about the wine?
Let my partner handle it.

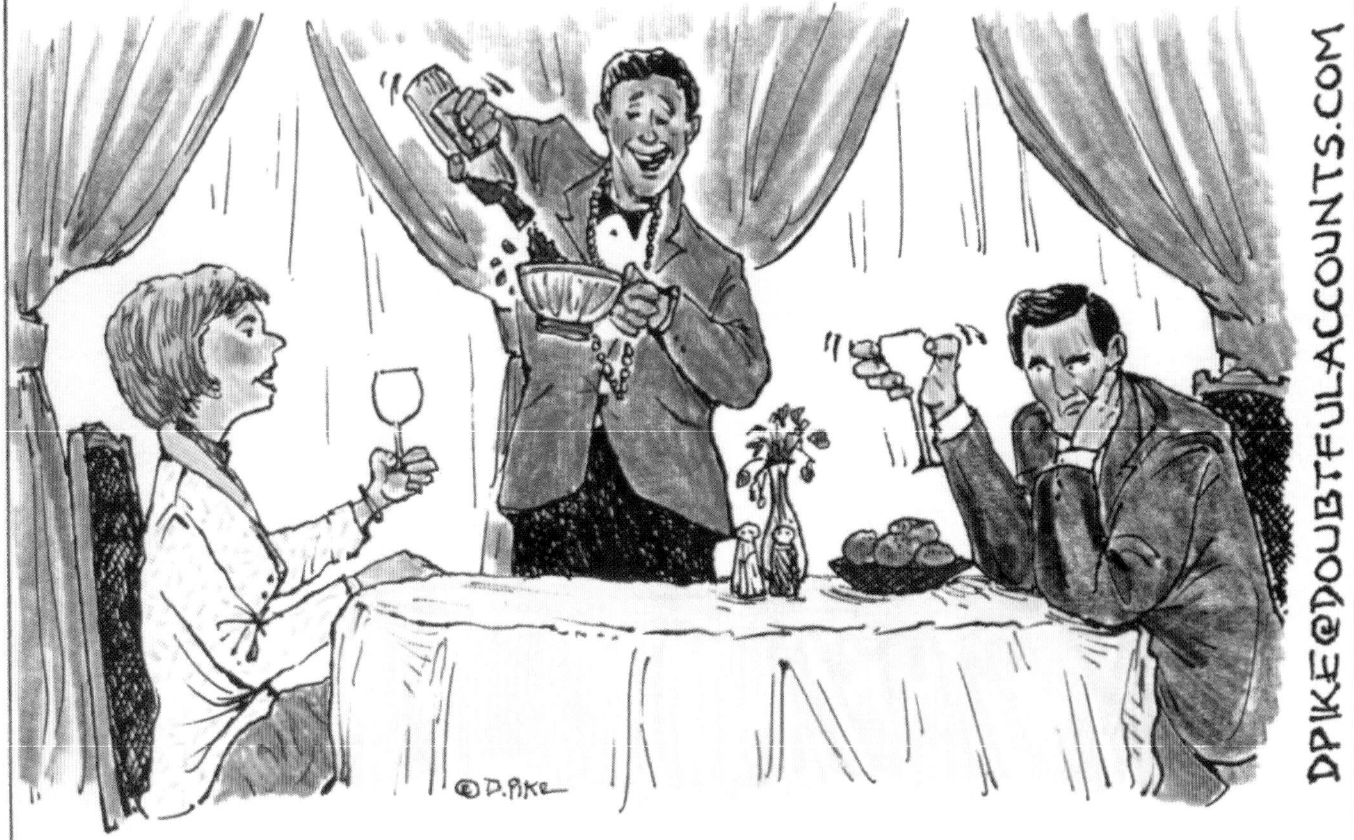
©D.Pike
DPIKE@DOUBTFULACCOUNTS.COM

Never trust a sommelier with a 750ml tastevin.

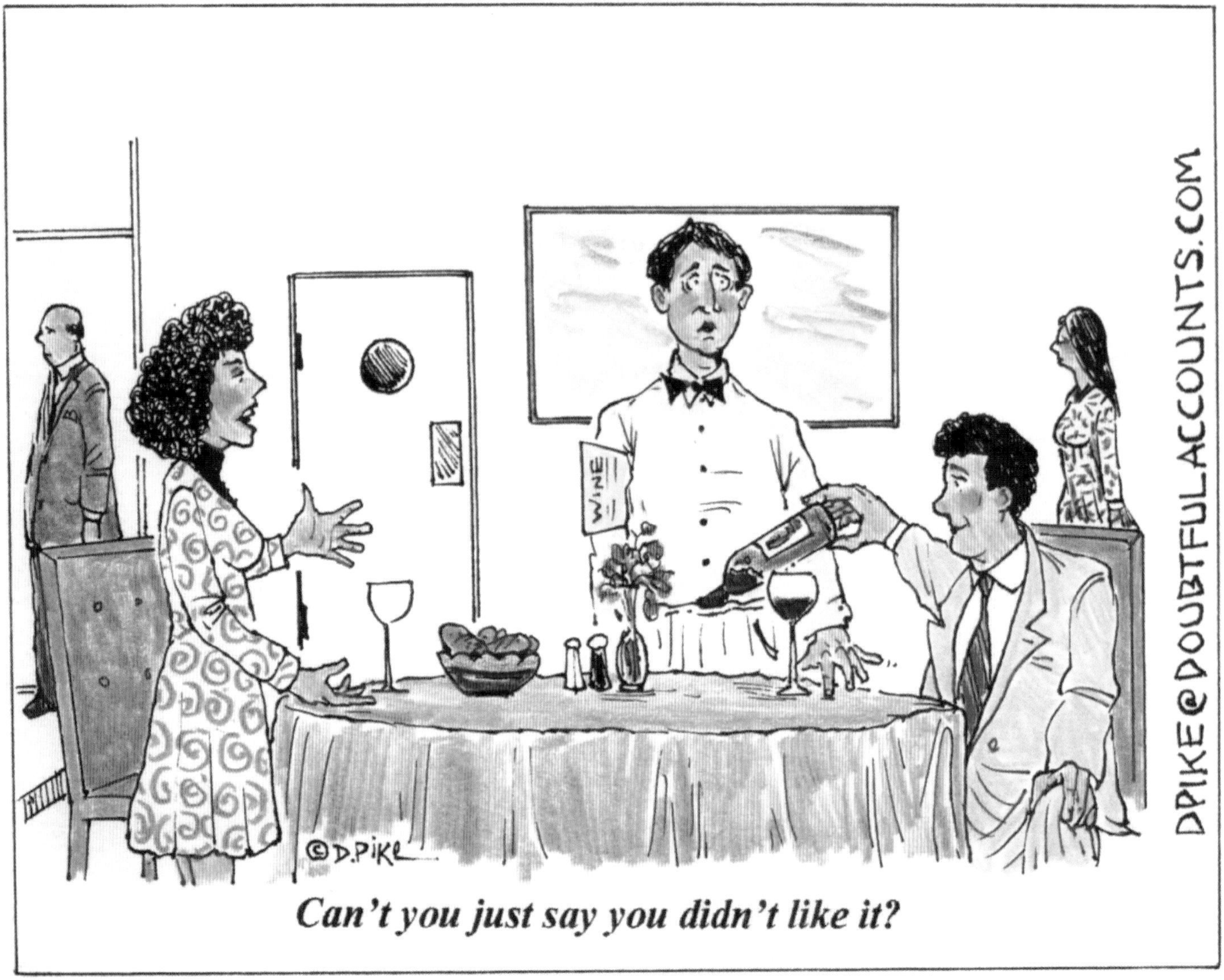
WINE
©D.PIKE
DPIKE@DOUBTFULACCOUNTS.COM

Can't you just say you didn't like it?

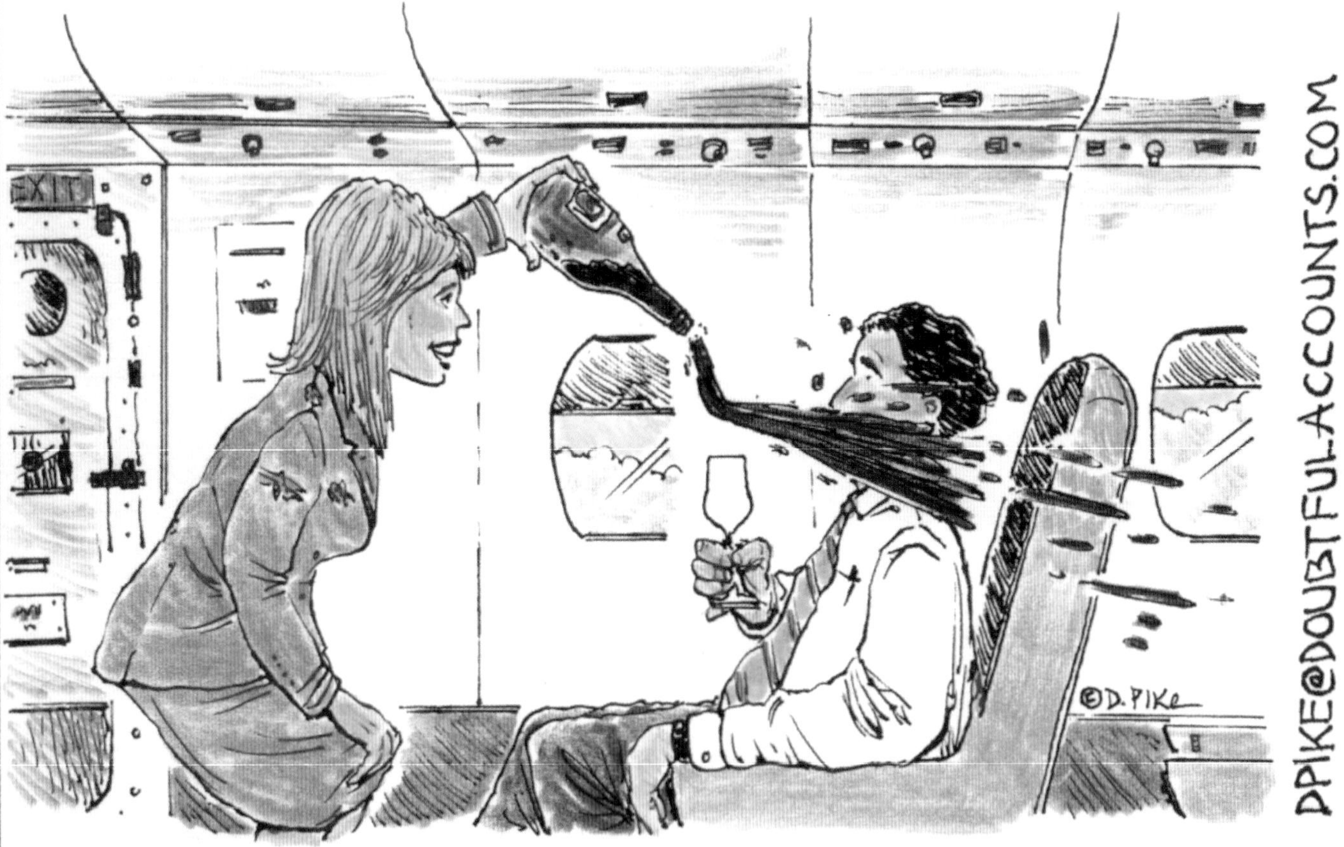
EXIT
©D. PIKE
DPIKE@DOUBTFULACCOUNTS.COM

Do you still want to hear why we don't pour during takeoff?

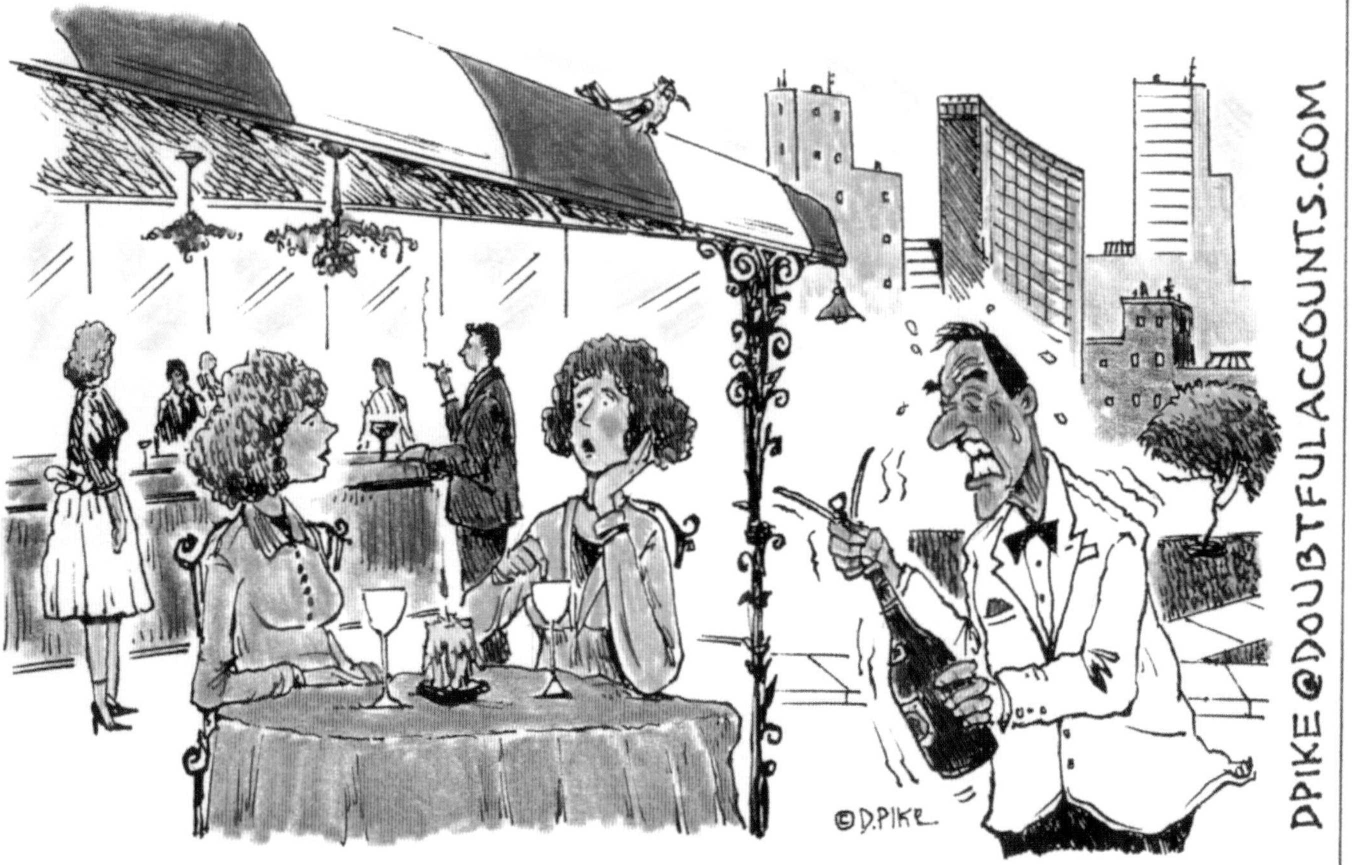
©D.PIKE
DPIKE@DOUBTFULACCOUNTS.COM

By the time he opens the Beaujolais, it's going to be an Old-o instead of a Nouveau.

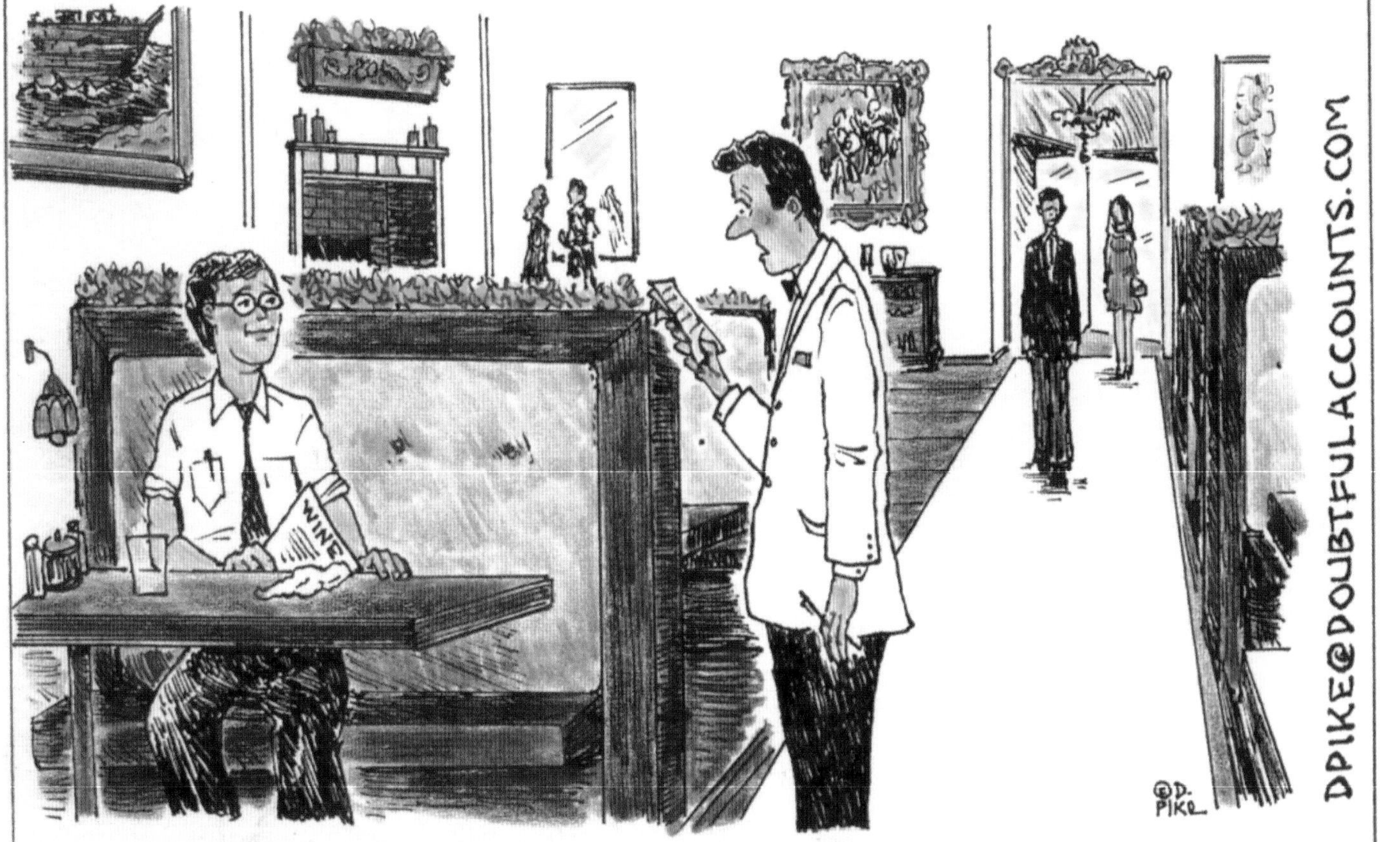
WINE
©D. PIKE
DPIKE@DOUBTFULACCOUNTS.COM

So it's the Mumm's Cordon Rouge, '98 Pouilly-Fuisse, '86 Chateau Margaux, and the '92 Barsac—would you like any food?

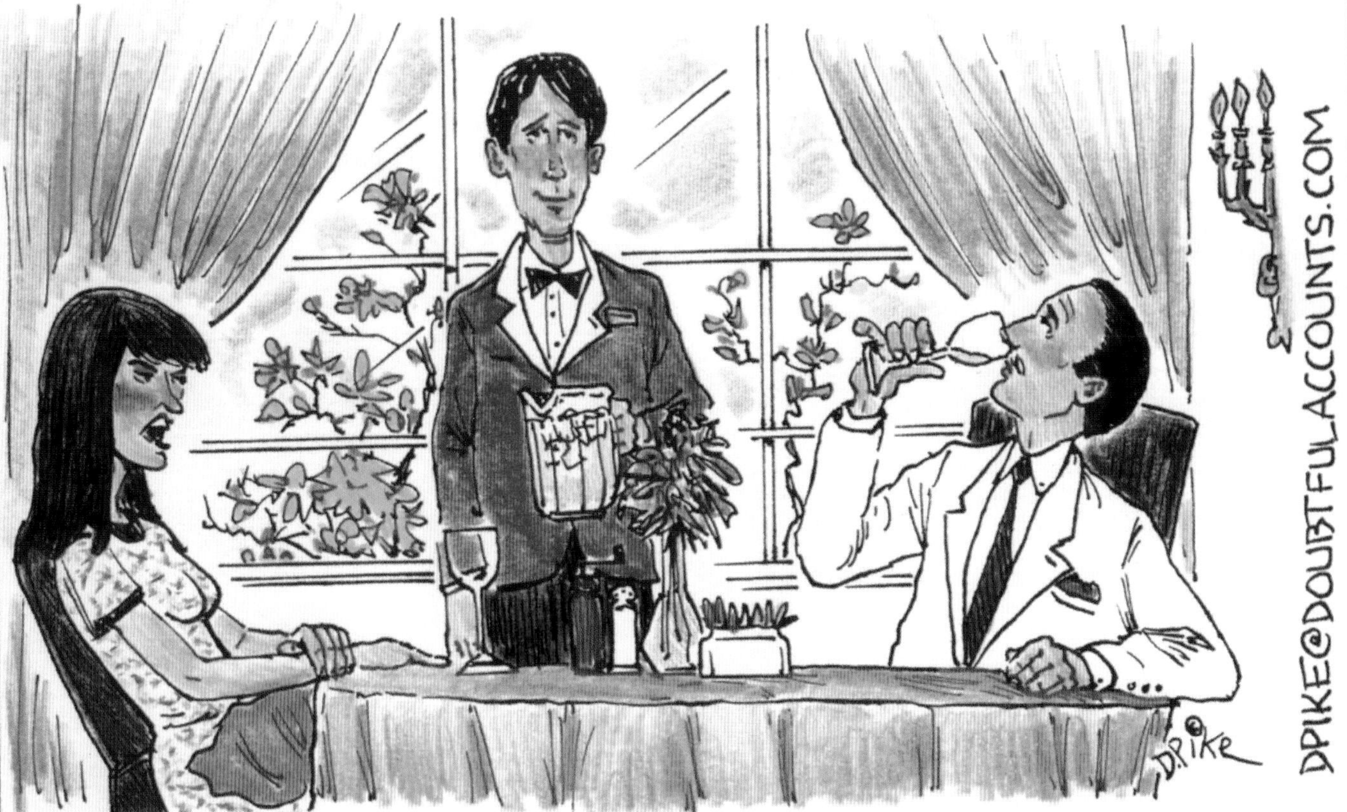
DPIKE@DOUBTFULACCOUNTS.COM
D.Pike

Frank, it's water.

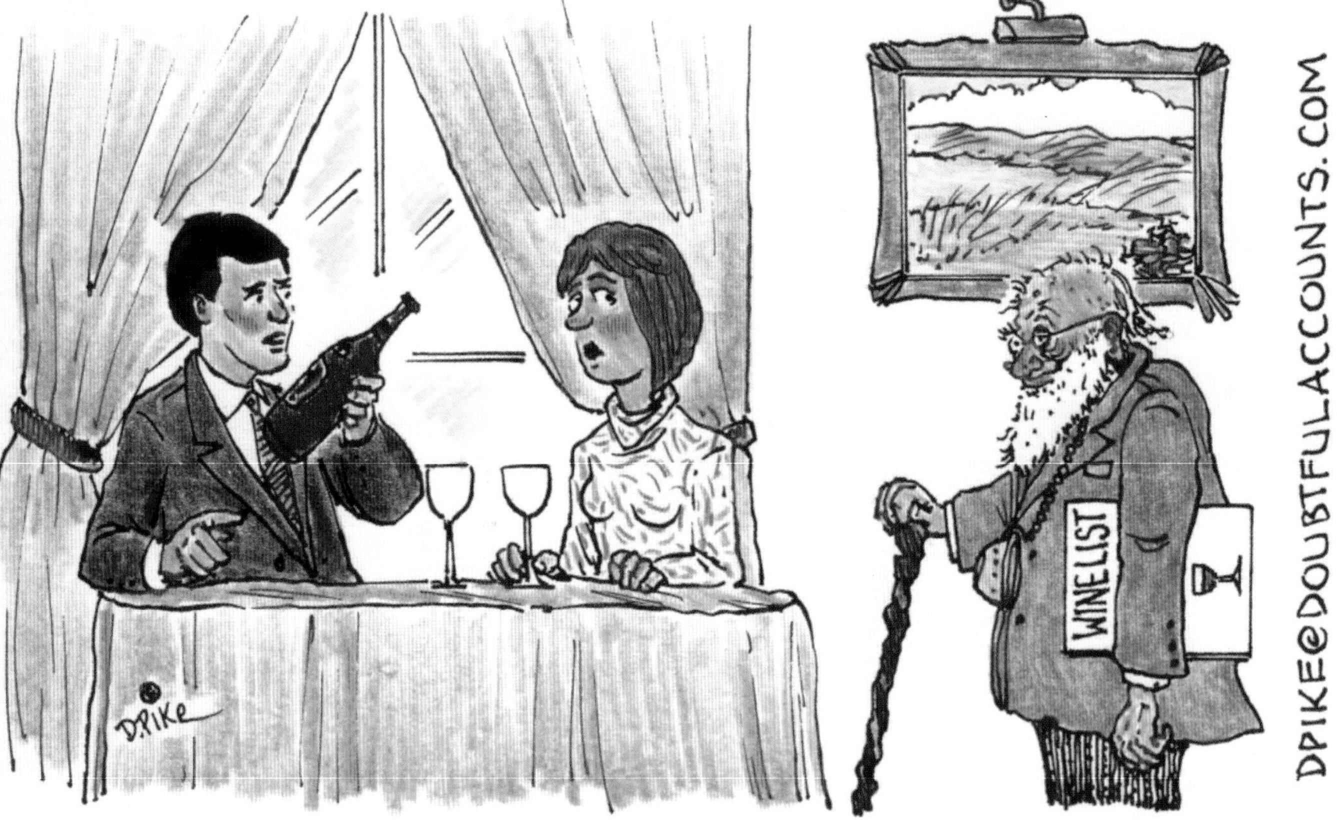
D.PIKE
WINELIST
DPIKE@DOUBTFULACCOUNTS.COM

The wine isn't pre-phylloxera, but I'm willing to bet the sommelier is.

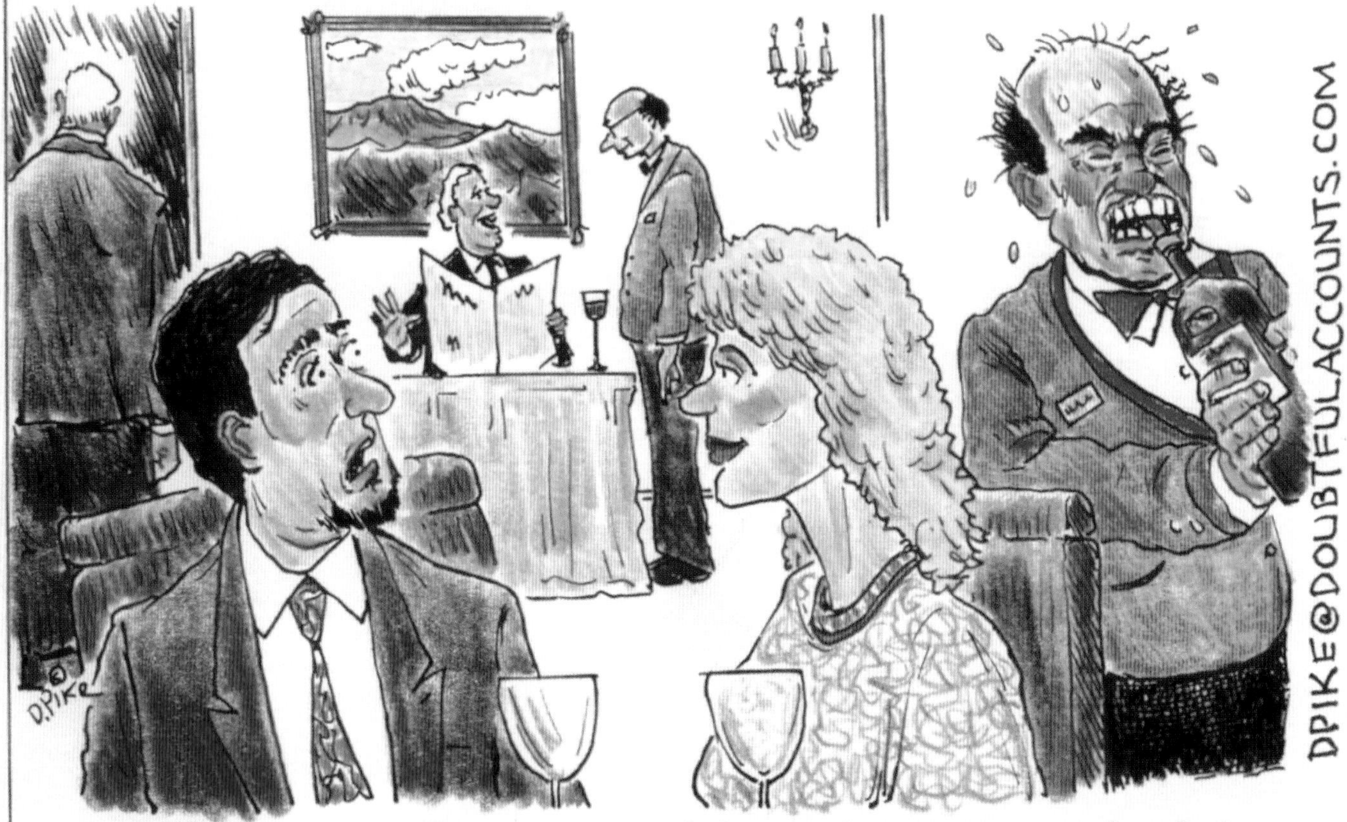
DPIKE@DOUBTFULACCOUNTS.COM
© D.PIKE

As I was saying, the opening of the modern screwcap bottle just doesn't have the same glamour as opening a cork-finished bottle.

4

Ben Hermitage:
The Winemaker at Work

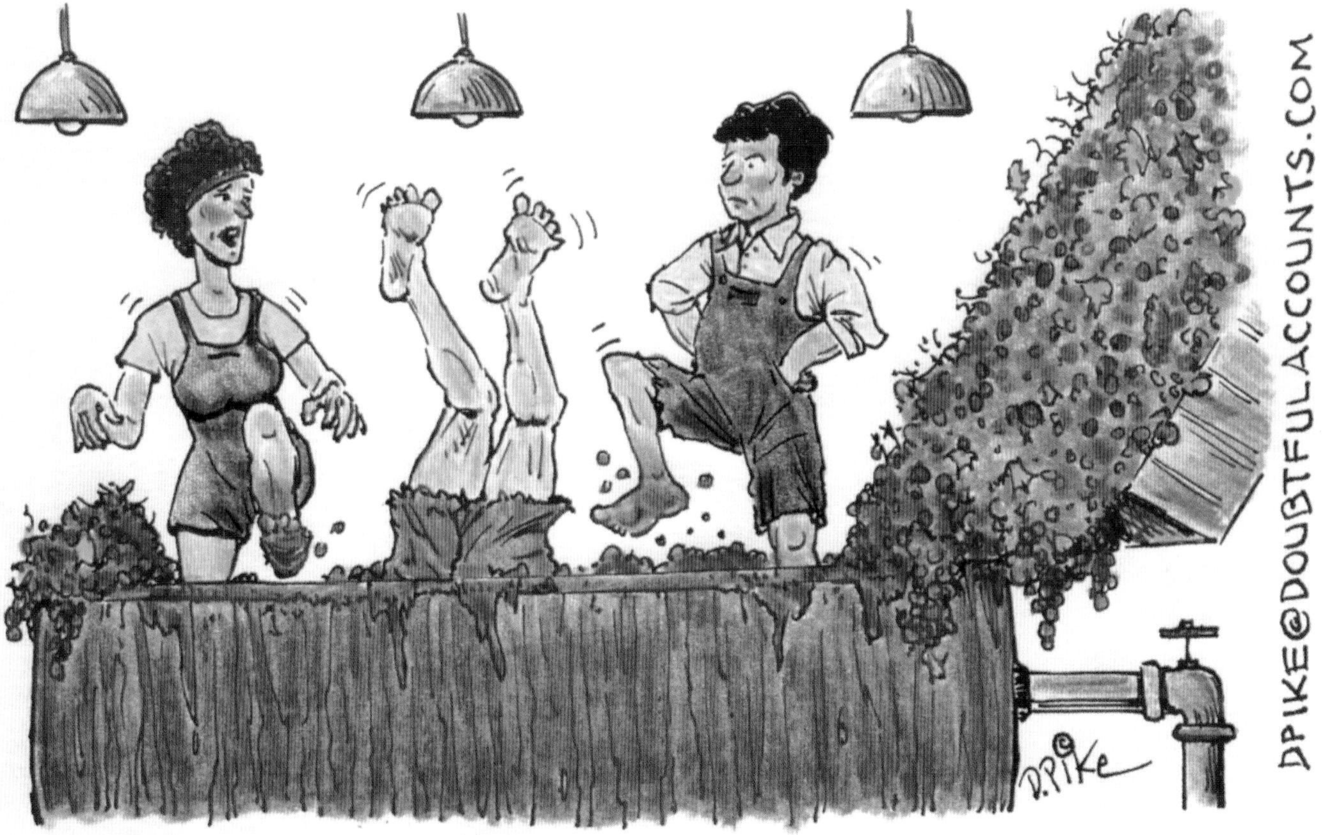
DPIKE@DOUBTFULACCOUNTS.COM
D.Pike ©

Who's the new guy?

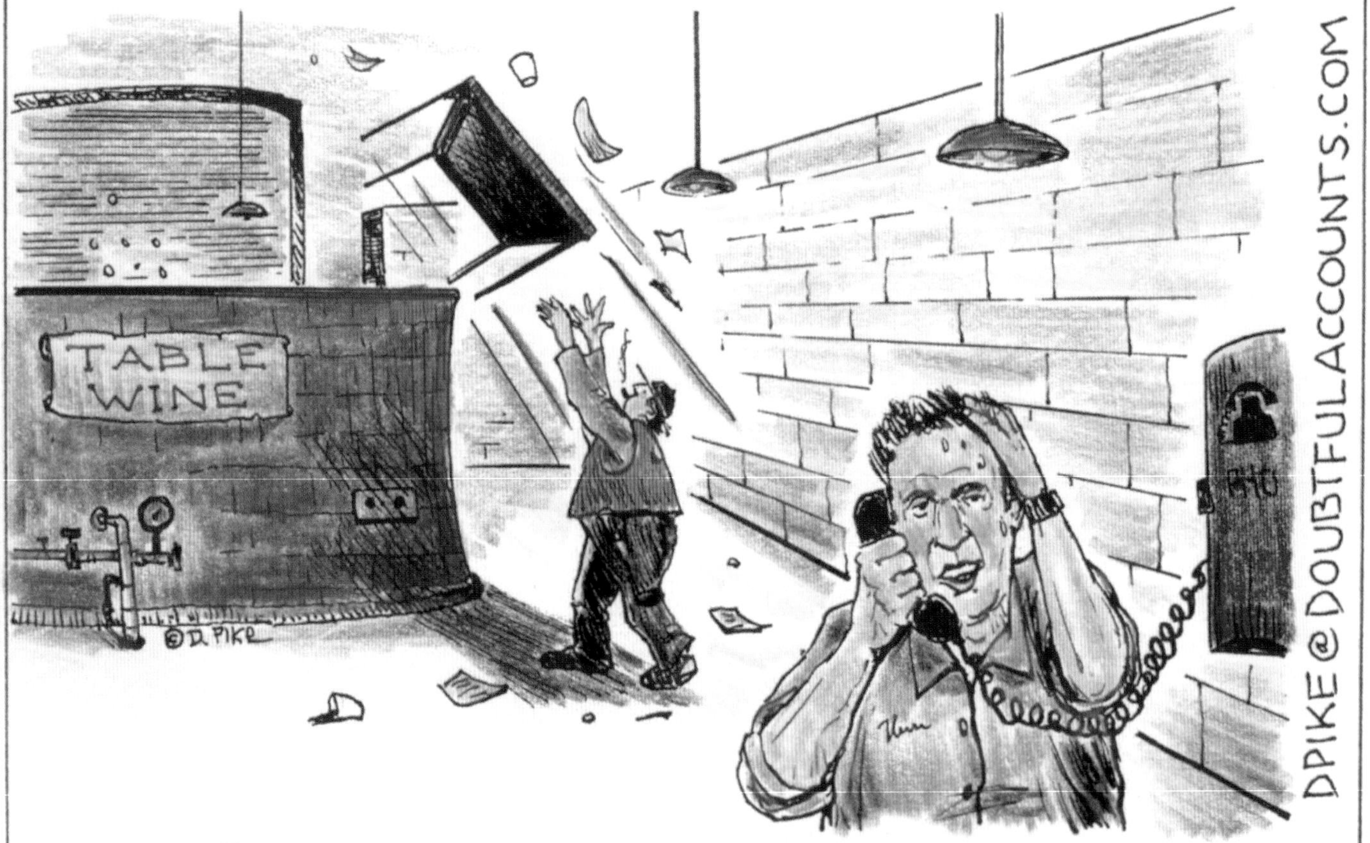
TABLE
WINE
©D. PIKE
DPIKE@DOUBTFULACCOUNTS.COM

Yeah, I've got the new guy working on table wines.
He seems to be getting the hang of it.

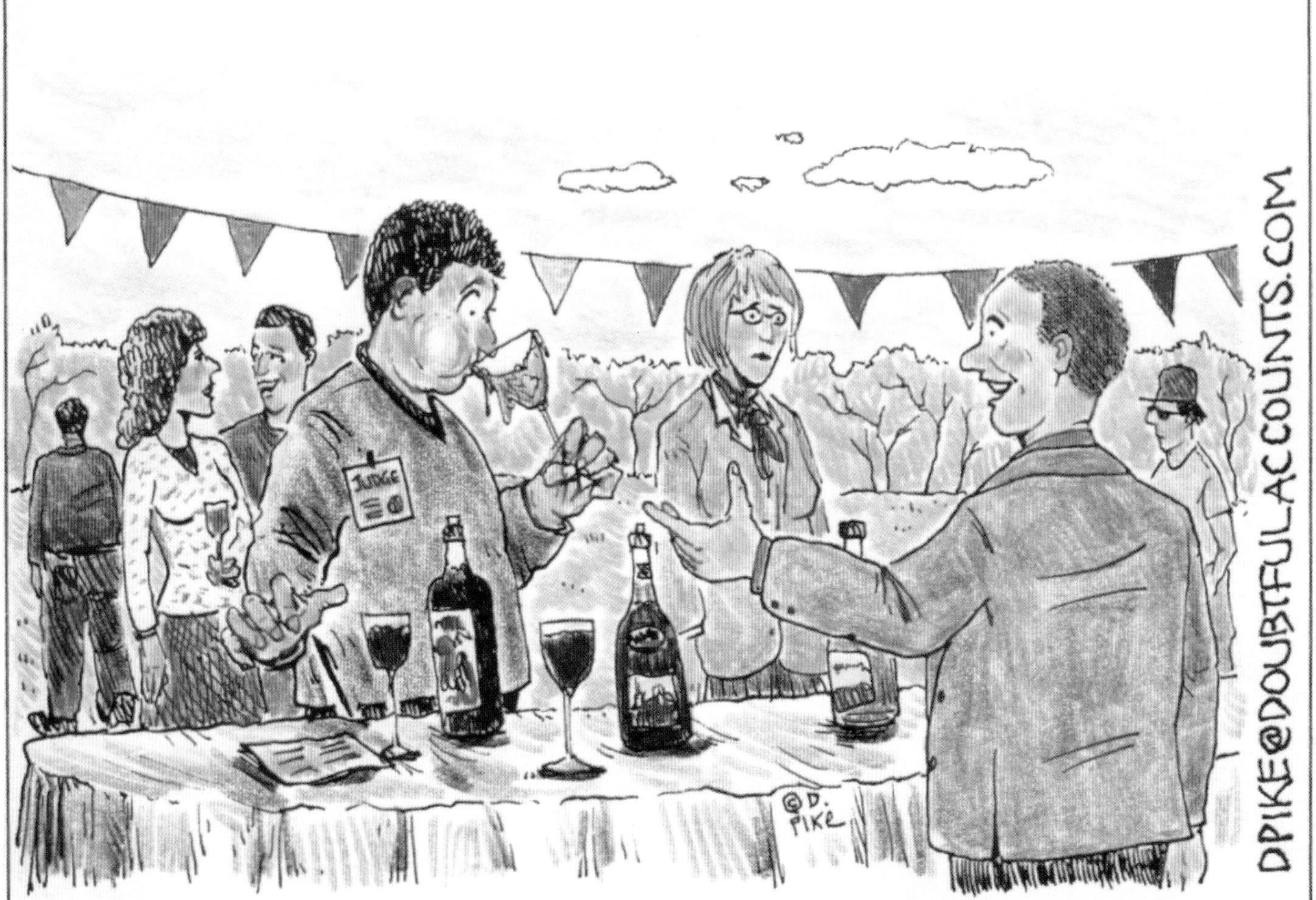
JUDGE
©D. PIKE
DPIKE@DOUBTFULACCOUNTS.COM

The merlot is 100% merlot; the pinot noir is 100% pinot noir, and the chardonnay is 100% Swiss chard.

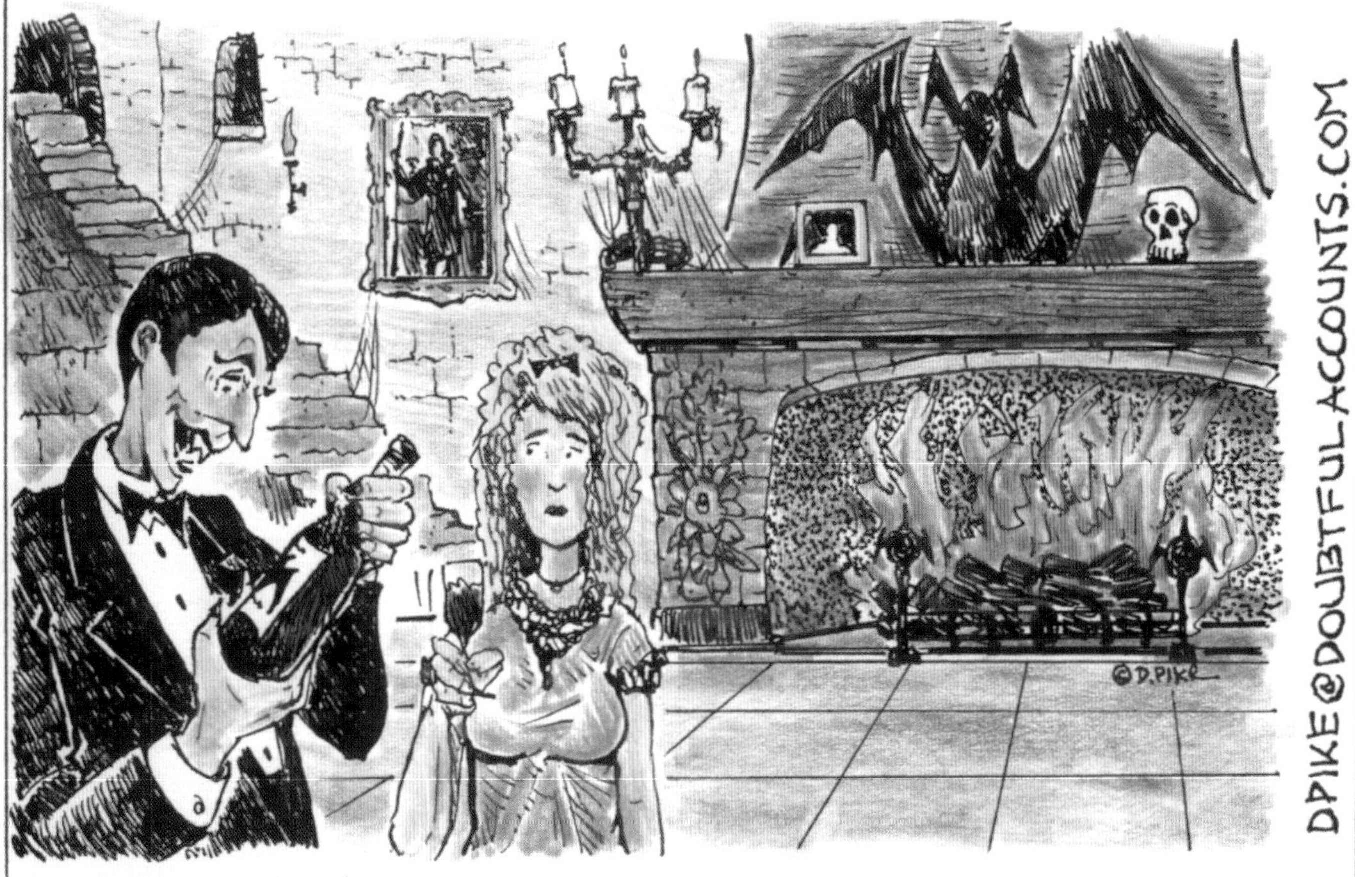
©D.PIKE
DPIKE@DOUBTFULACCOUNTS.COM

It's a little varietal I bottle myself...Type A positive.

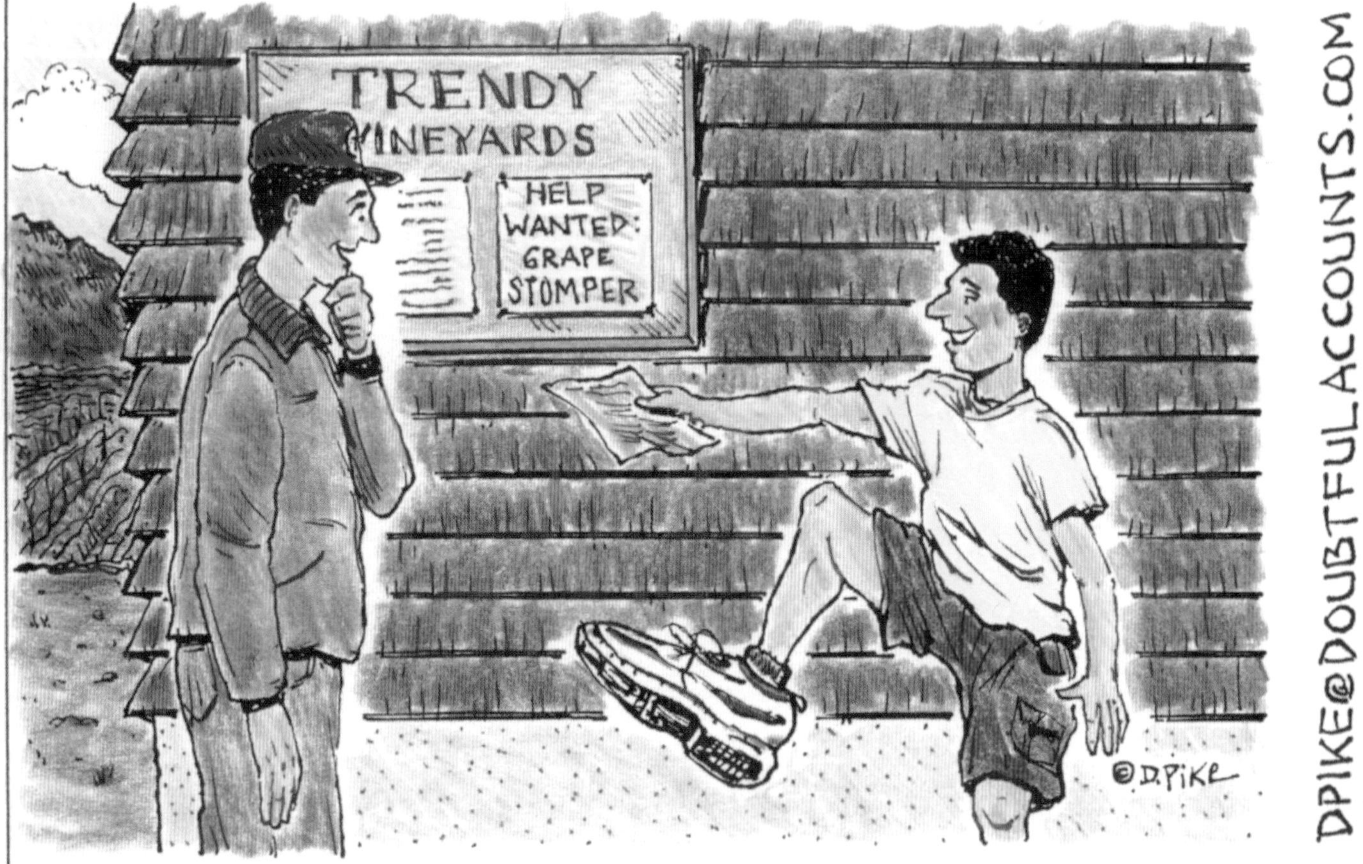
TRENDY
INEYARDS
HELP
WANTED:
GRAPE
STOMPER
©D.PIKE
DPIKE@DOUBTFULACCOUNTS.COM

I think we can skip the résumé.

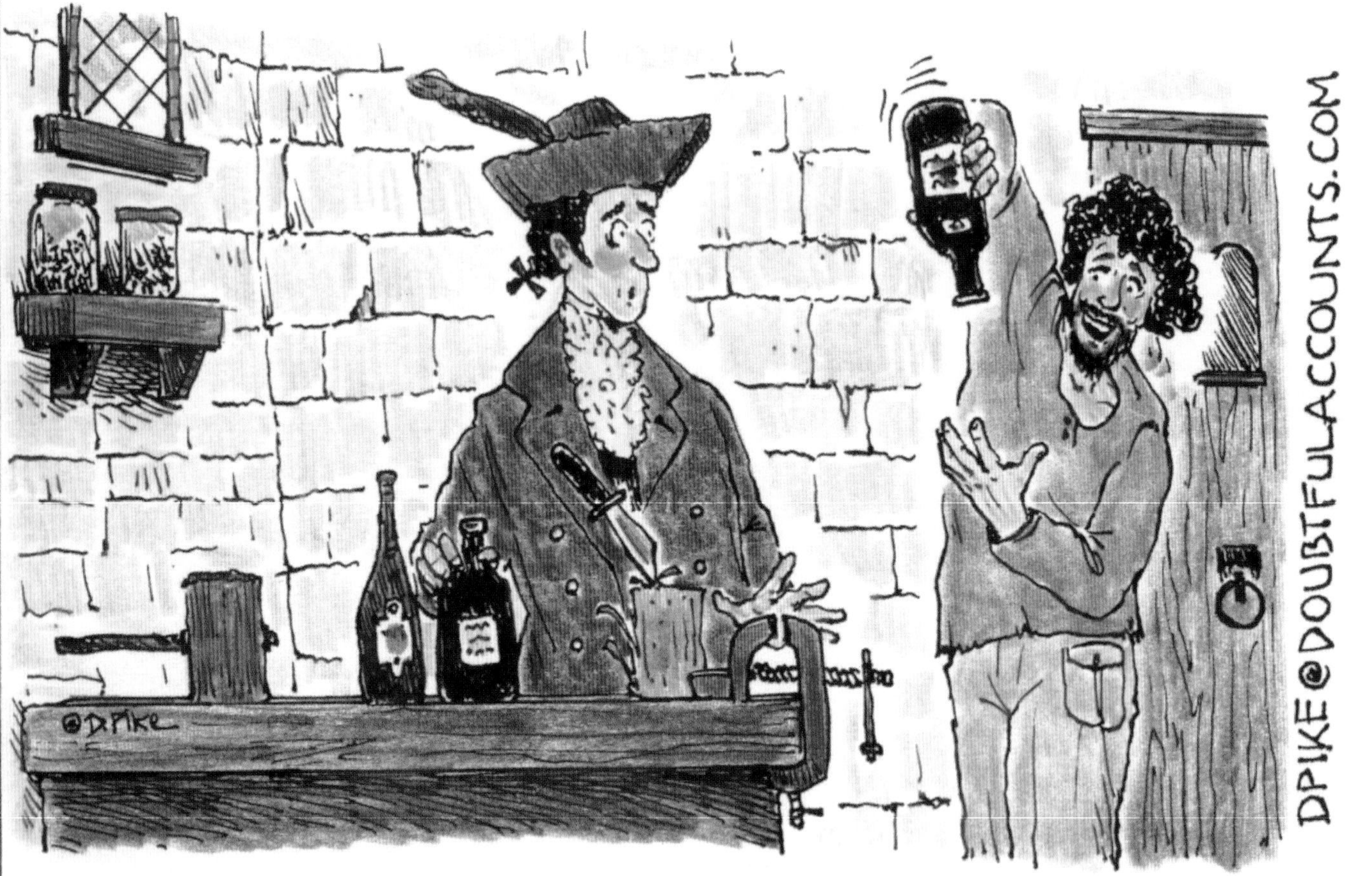
©D.Pike
DPIKE@DOUBTFULACCOUNTS.COM

This cork idea of yours is great! How do you get it out?

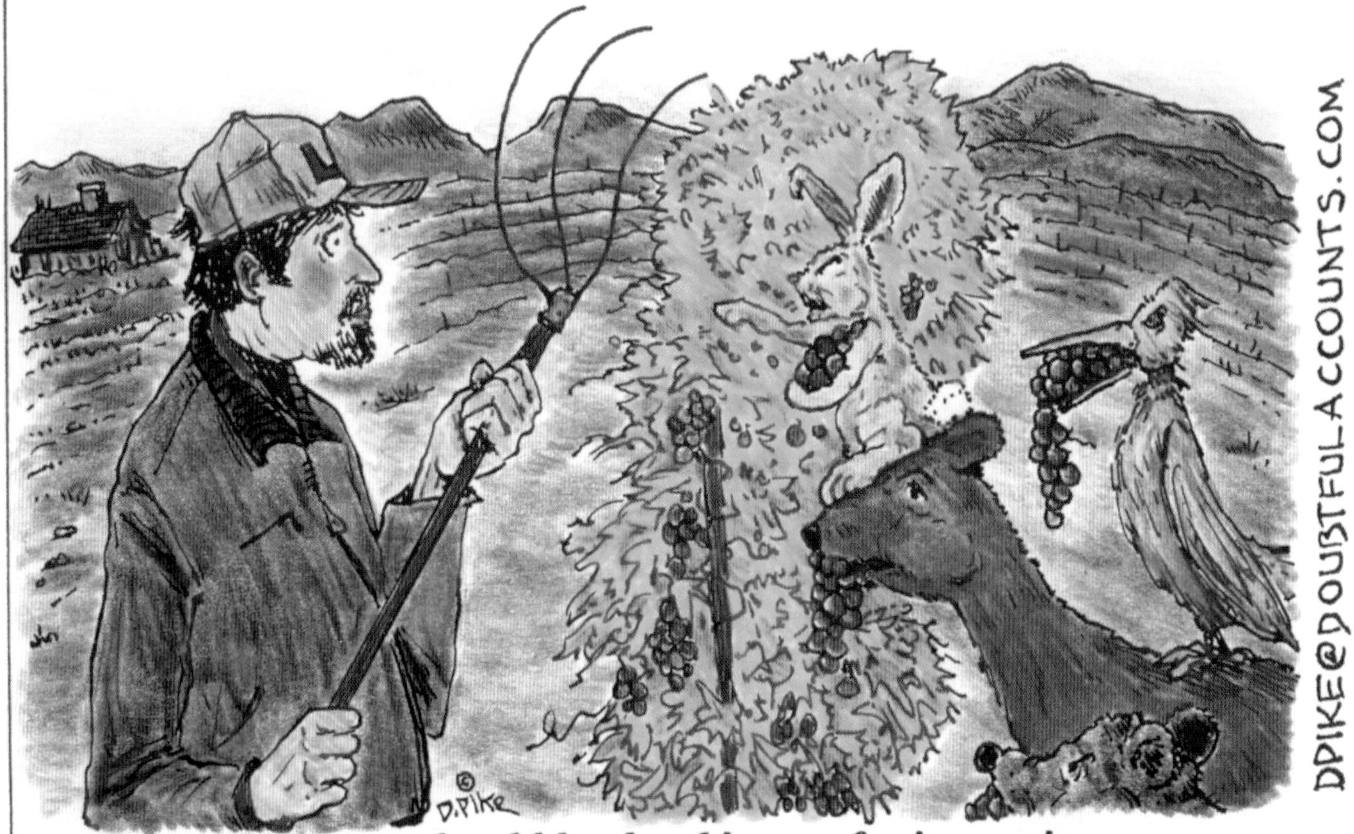
© D.Pike
DPIKE@DOUBTFULACCOUNTS.COM

Hey, you should be thanking us for improving your cluster-to-leaf balance.

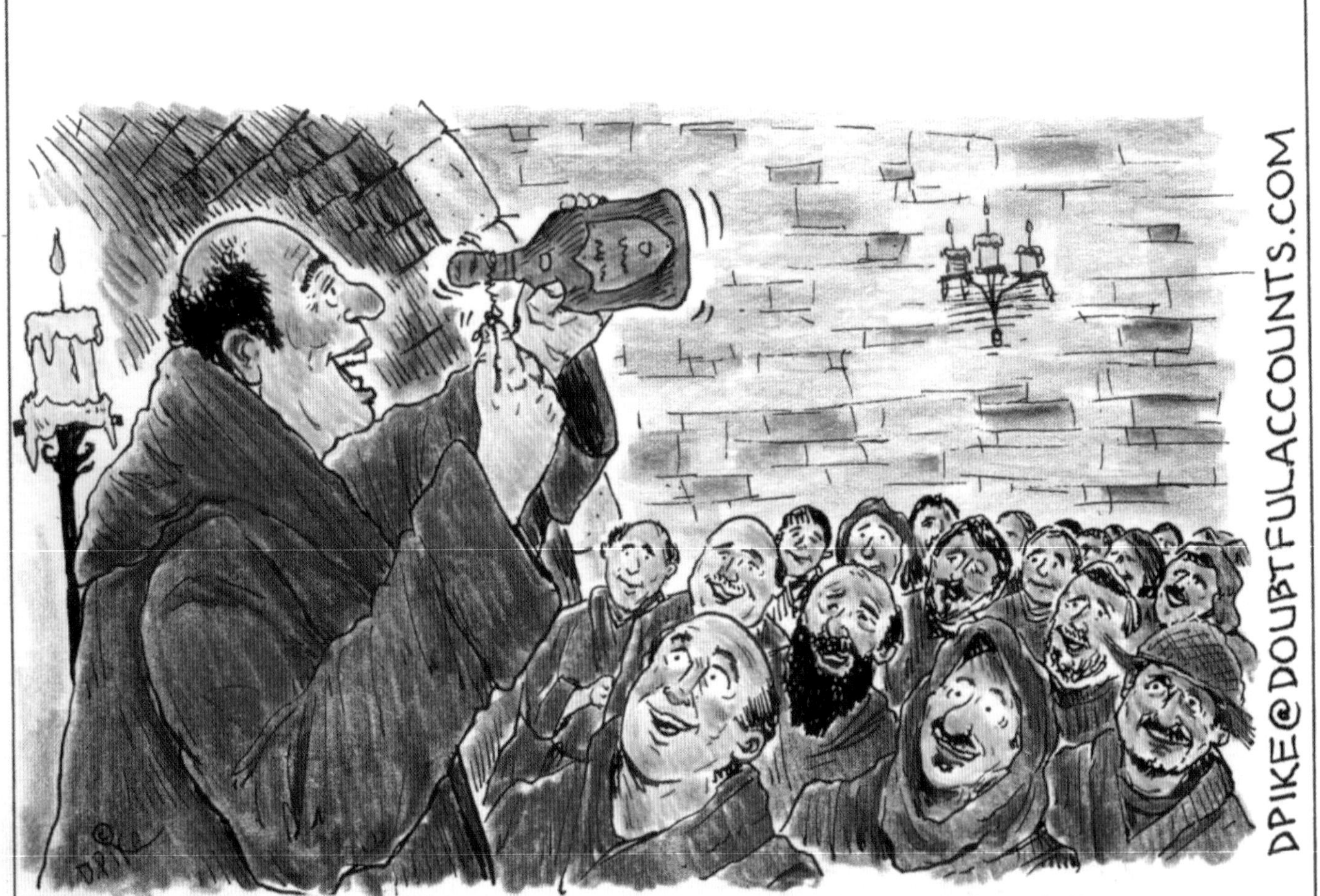
DPIKE@DOUBTFULACCOUNTS.COM

I, Dom Perignon, will now uncork the very first bottle of Champagne. Of course, I'm just guessing this is the right way to do it.

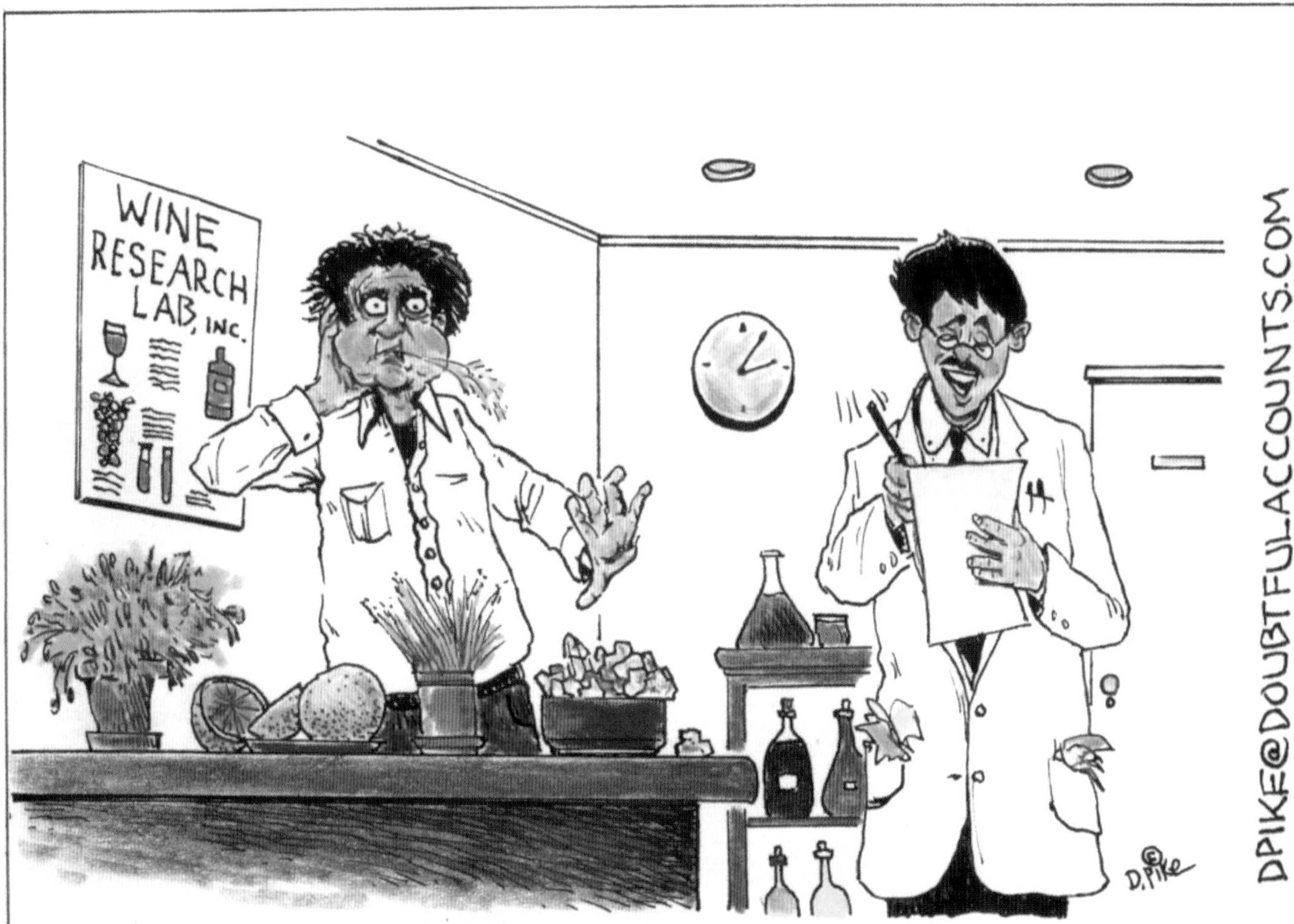
WINE
RESEARCH
LAB, INC.
DPIKE@DOUBTFULACCOUNTS.COM
© D.Pike

Okay, you've got a mouthful of minerals, grapefruit, herbs and grass.
Is it starting to taste like a sauvignon blanc?

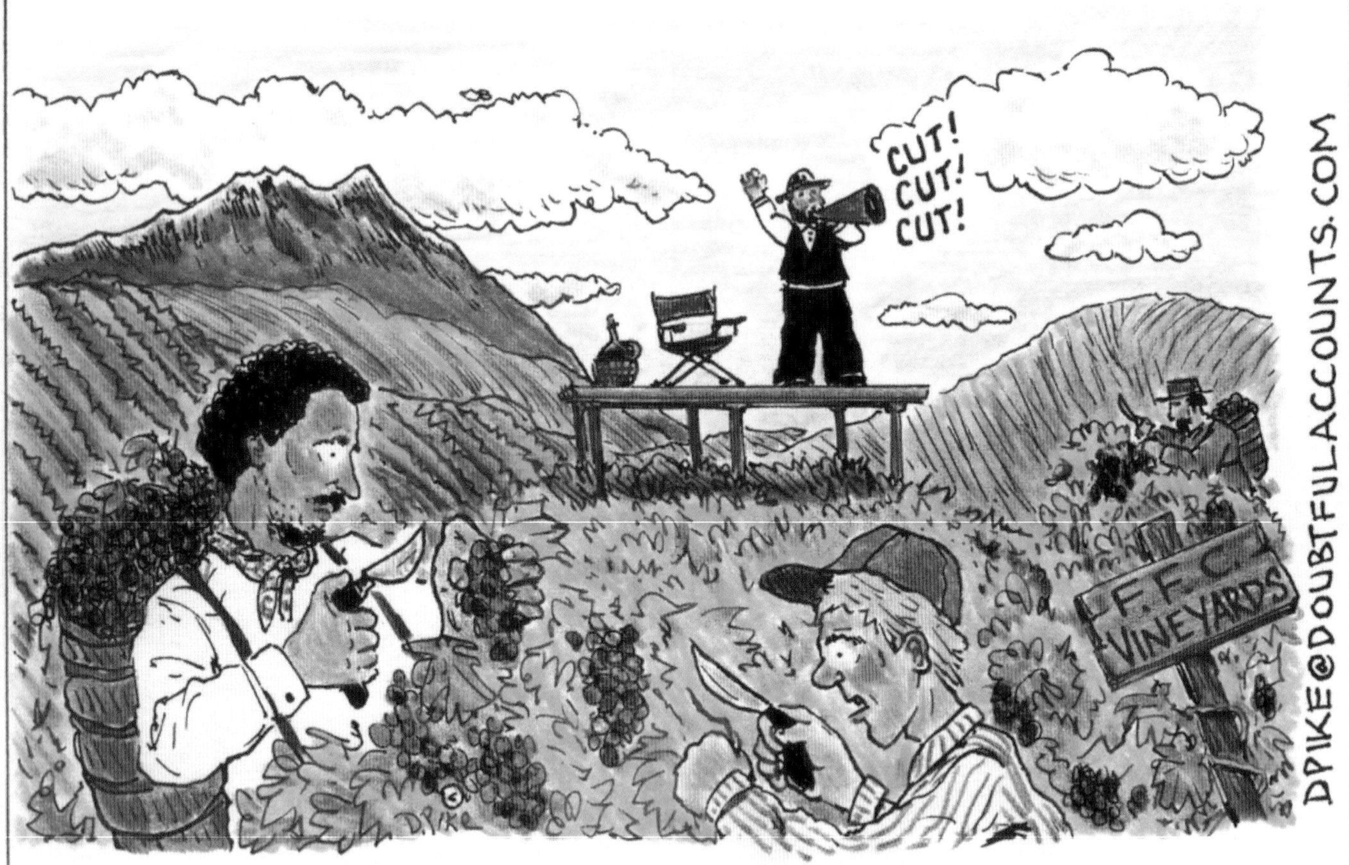
CUT!
CUT!
CUT!
F.F.C.
VINEYARDS
D.PIKE
DPIKE@DOUBTFULACCOUNTS.COM

Funny, when he was a movie director and yelled, "cut", he wanted everyone to stop.

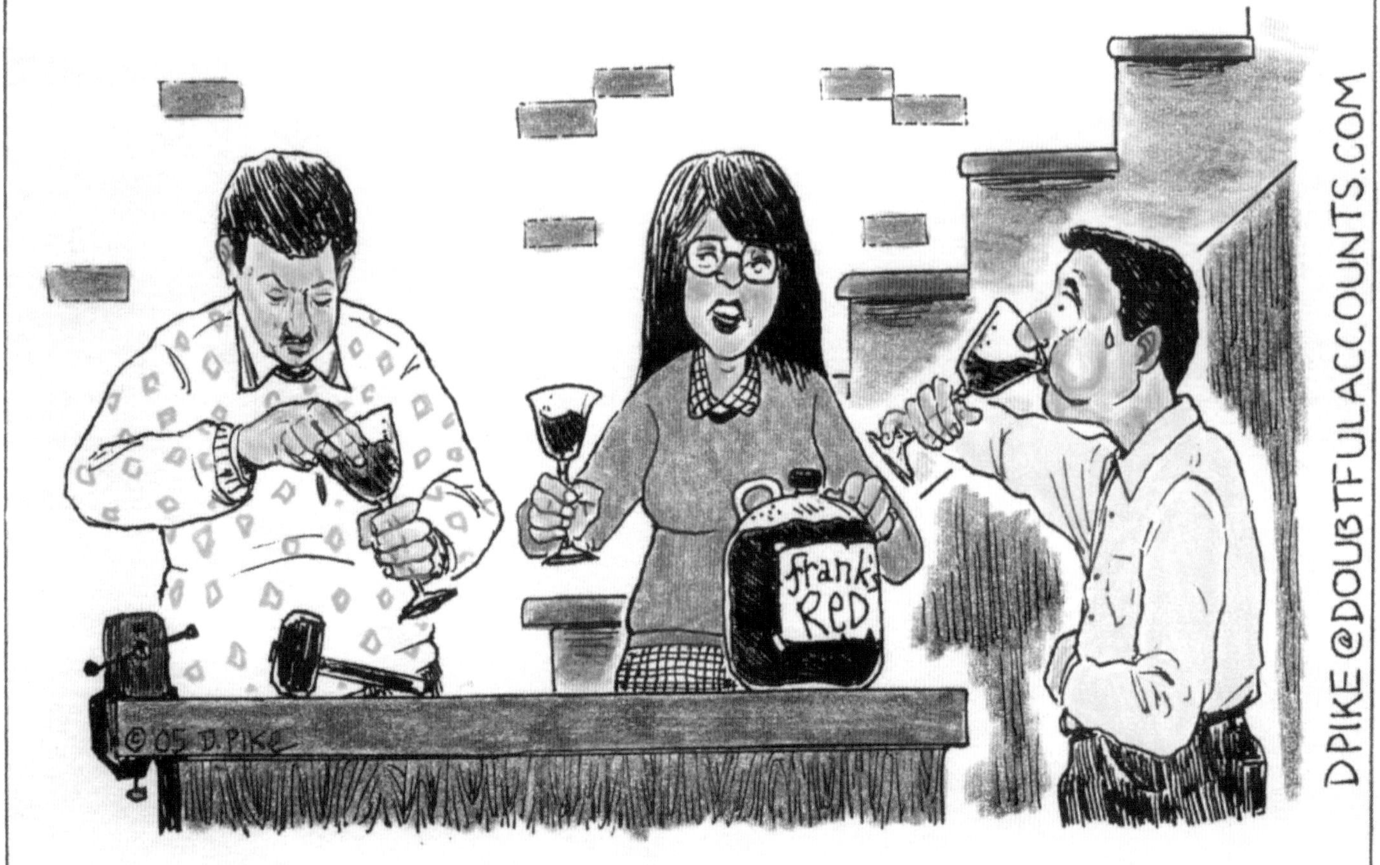
Frank's RED
© 05 D.PIKE
DPIKE@DOUBTFULACCOUNTS.COM

Frank makes it himself; it's the perfect wine—to serve with haggis.

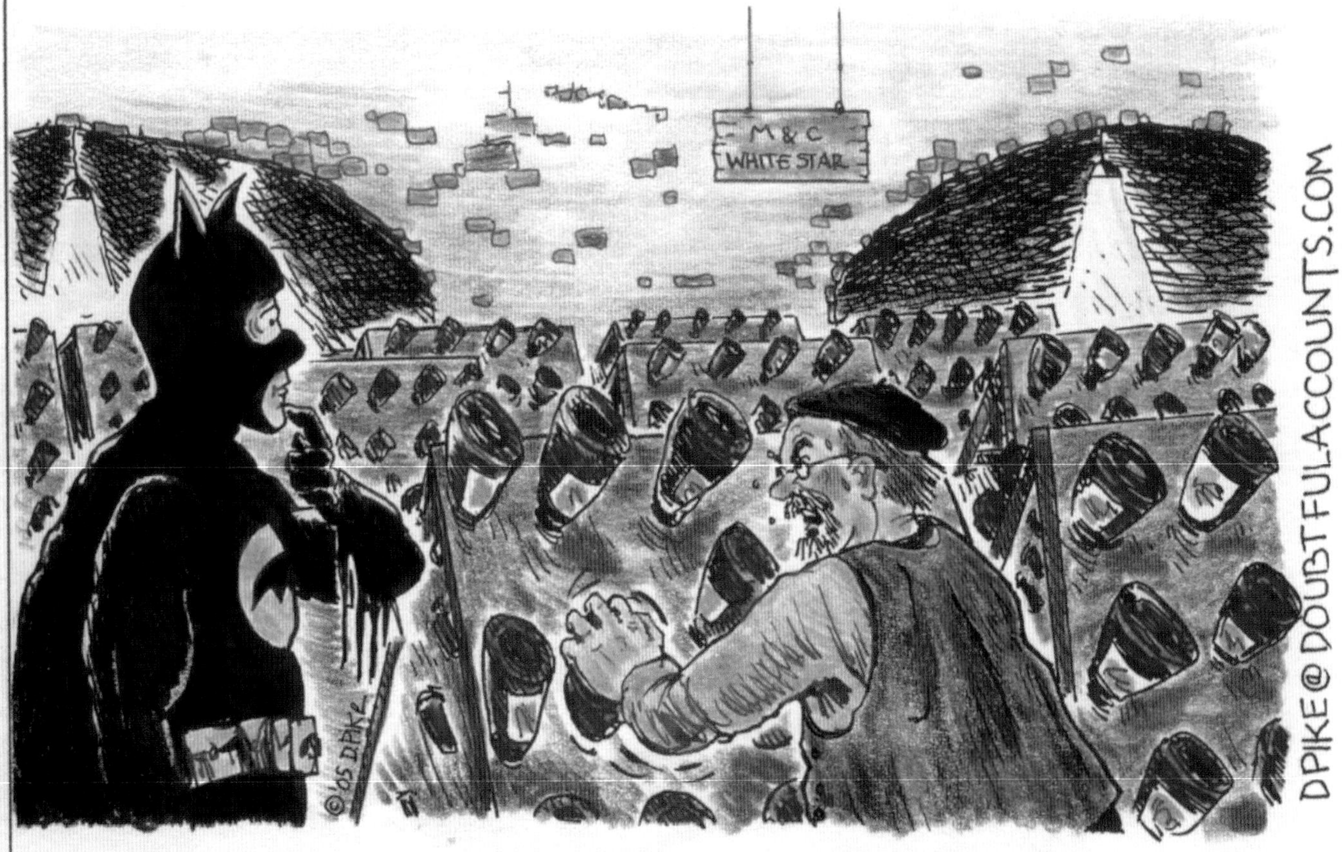
M & C
WHITE STAR
©05 DPIKE
DPIKE@DOUBTFULACCOUNTS.COM

Yeah, I'm the riddler—whadda ya want?

5

Saving Private Rhine Wine: The Domestic Front

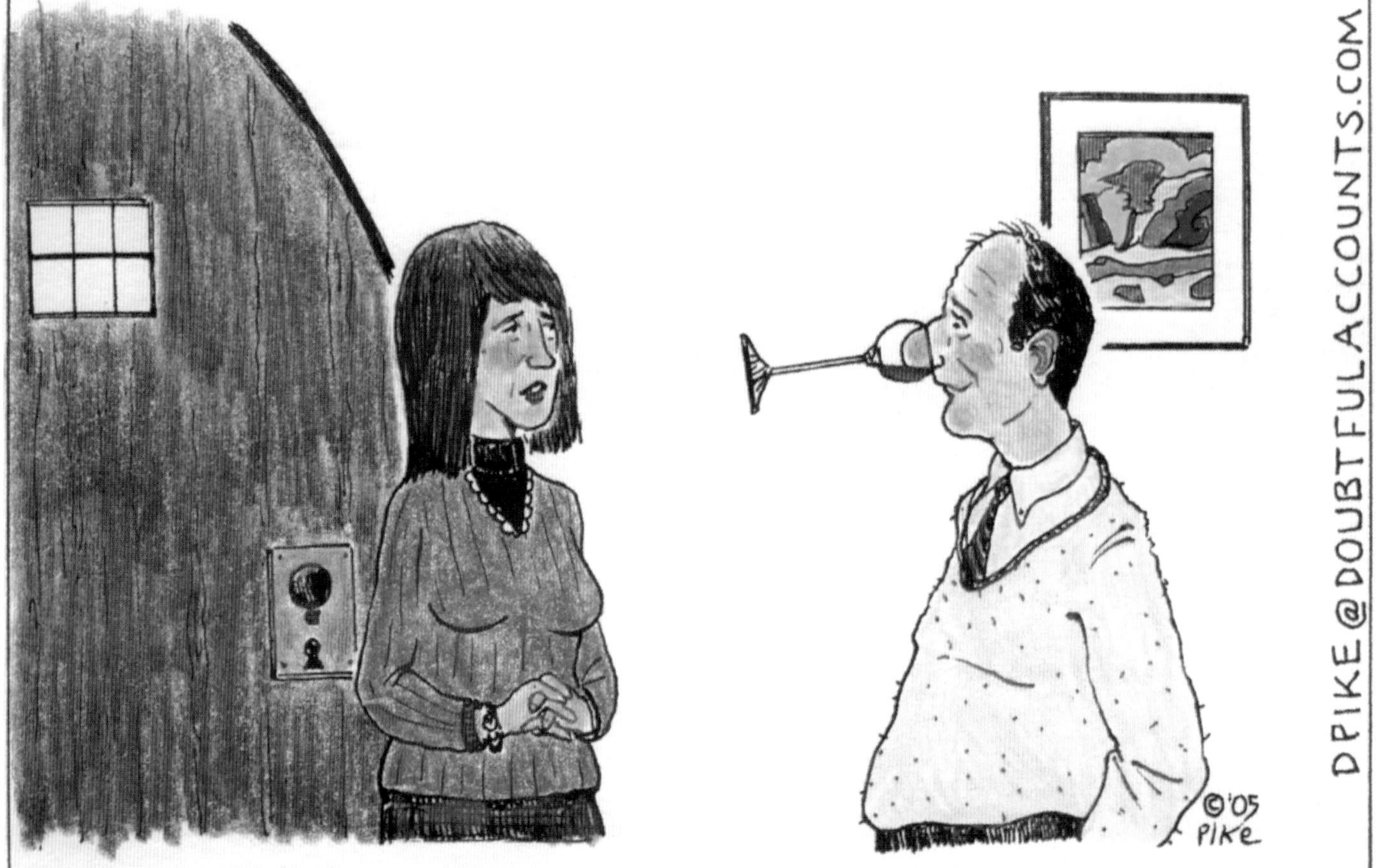
DPIKE@DOUBTFULACCOUNTS.COM
©'05
PIKE

I don't care how great the '61 Lafite is, Paul. You opened it in '97.

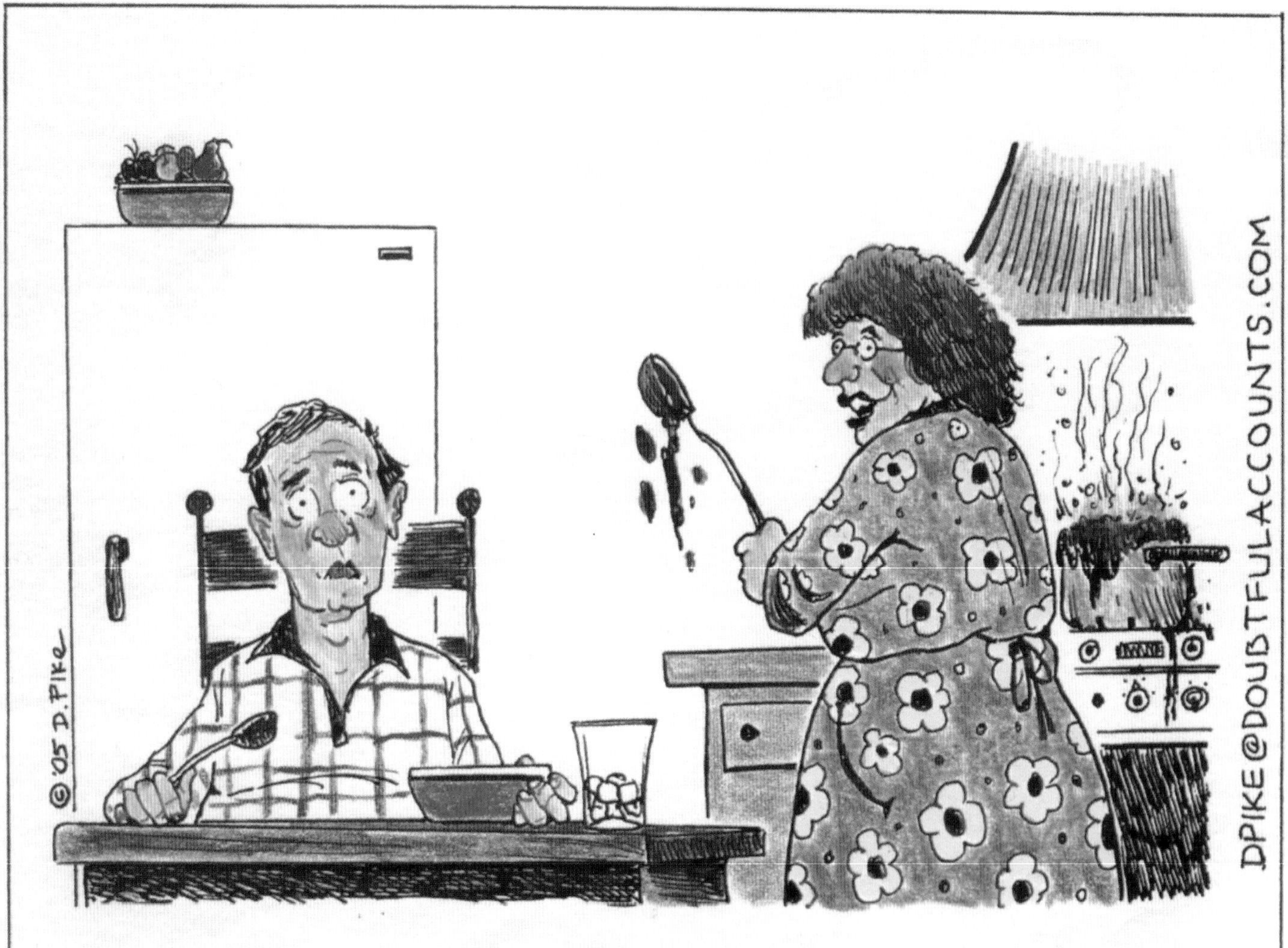
©'05 D. Pike
DPIKE@DOUBTFULACCOUNTS.COM

I knew you'd like the chili; I made it with your '45 Chateau Latour.

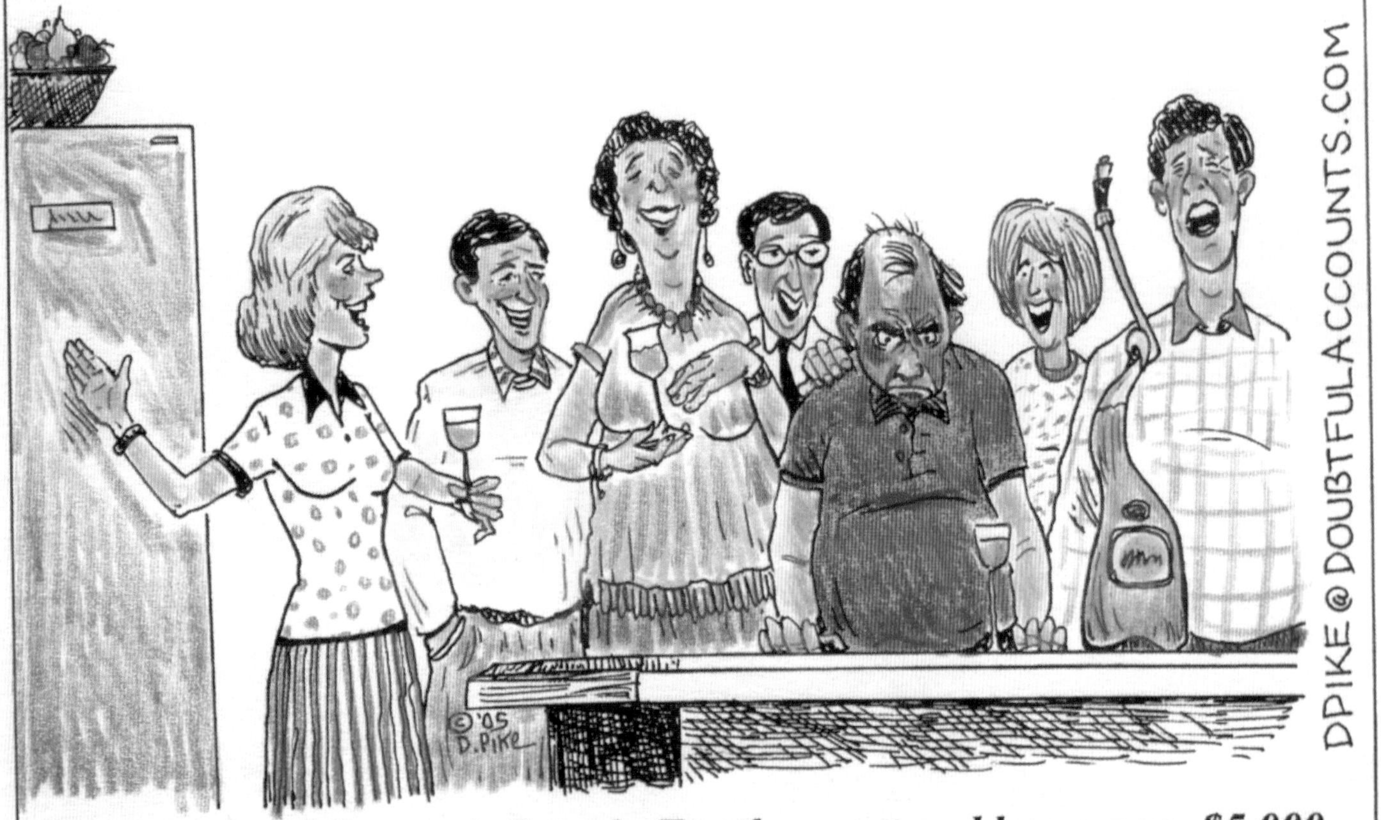
©'05
D.Pike
DPIKE@DOUBTFULACCOUNTS.COM

And the funniest part is I made Frank go out and buy a new, $5,000 fridge, just to hold a $4.00 bottle of wine!

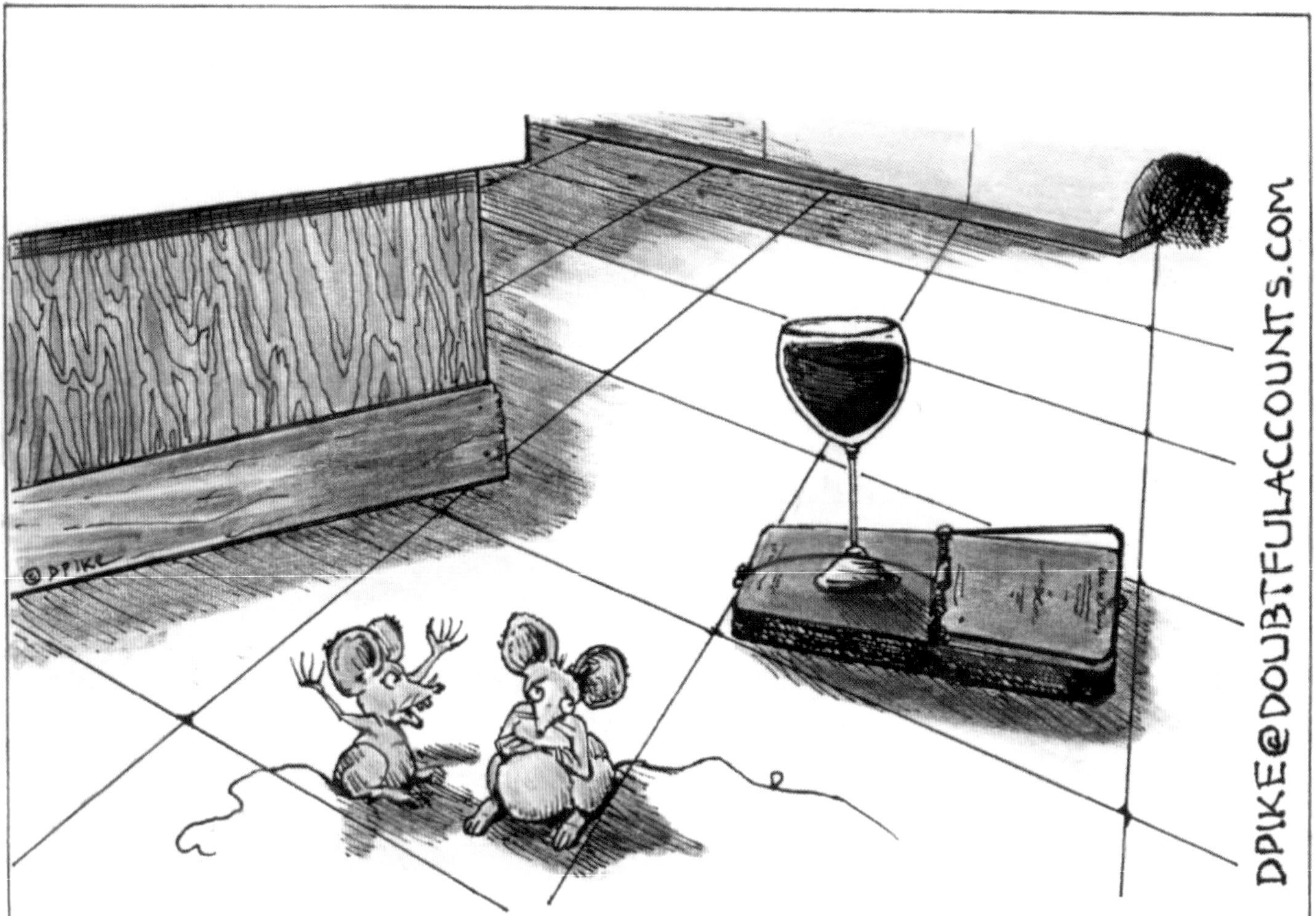
© DPIKE
DPIKE@DOUBTFULACCOUNTS.COM

No-o-o-o! Wisconsin wasn't good enough! You had to insist that we move to Napa Valley!

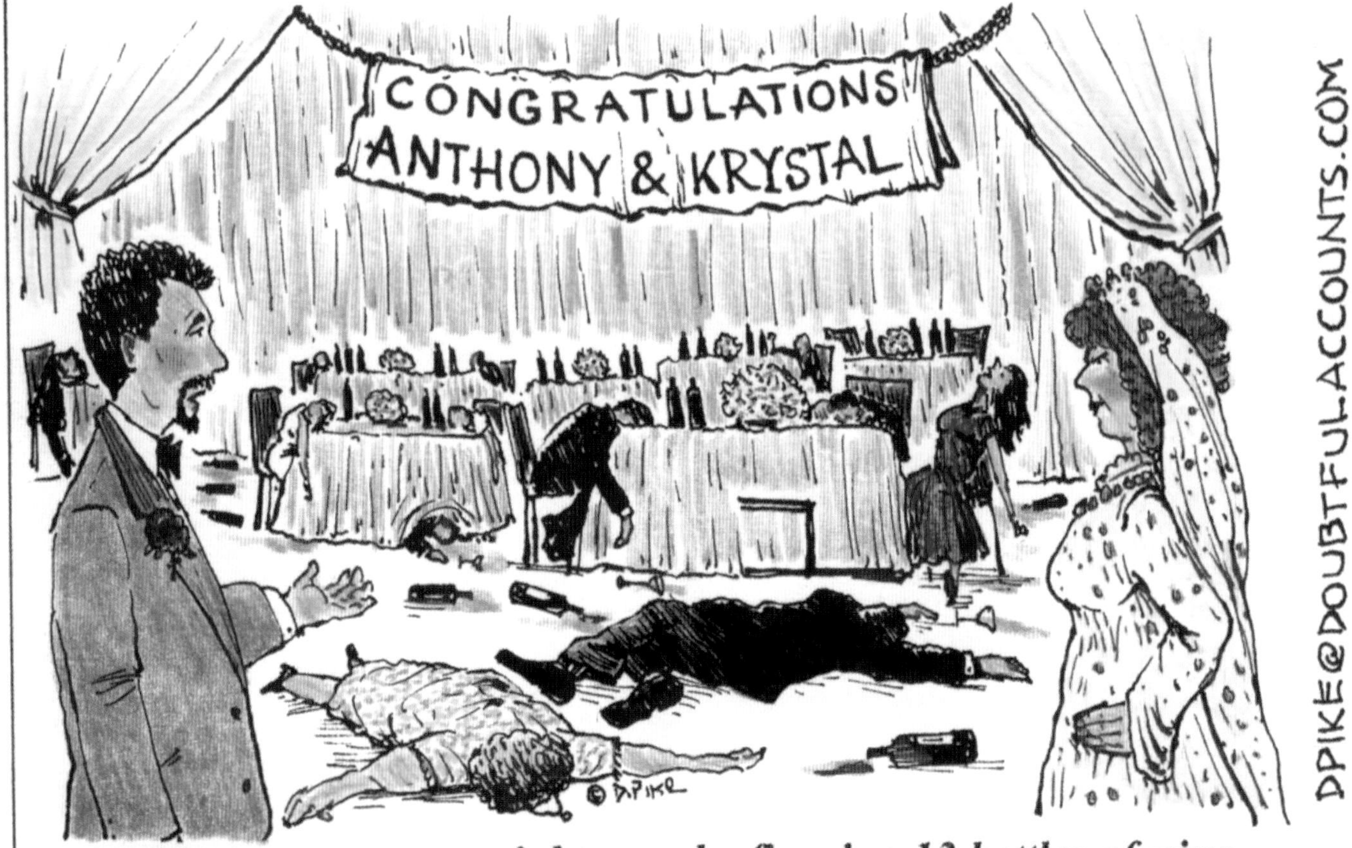
CONGRATULATIONS
ANTHONY & KRYSTAL
© D.PIKE
DPIKE@DOUBTFULACCOUNTS.COM

Okay, so you were right; maybe figuring 13 bottles of wine per person was a little too much.

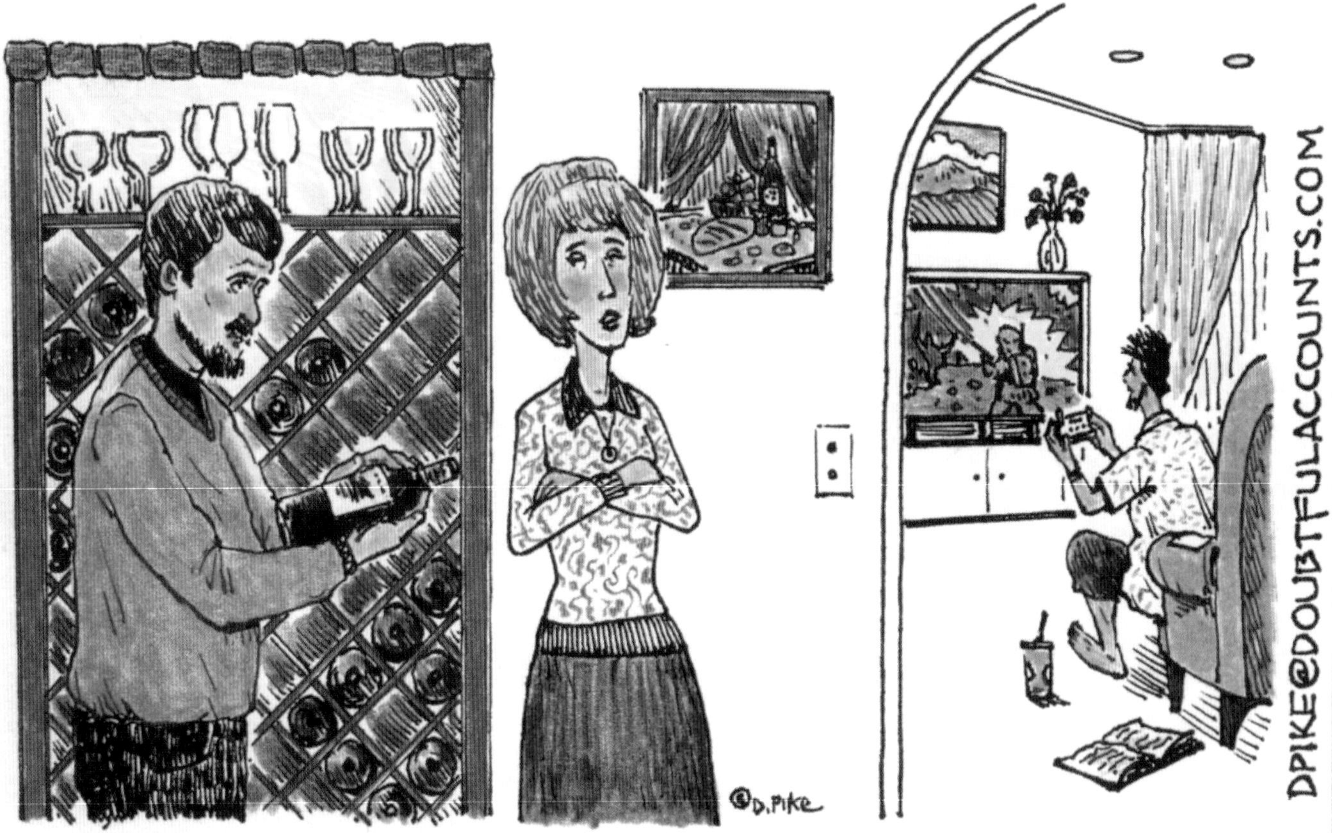
©D.Pike
DPIKE@DOUBTFULACCOUNTS.COM

You're laying down that bottle for when Rich graduates from college? Don't you ever want to drink it?

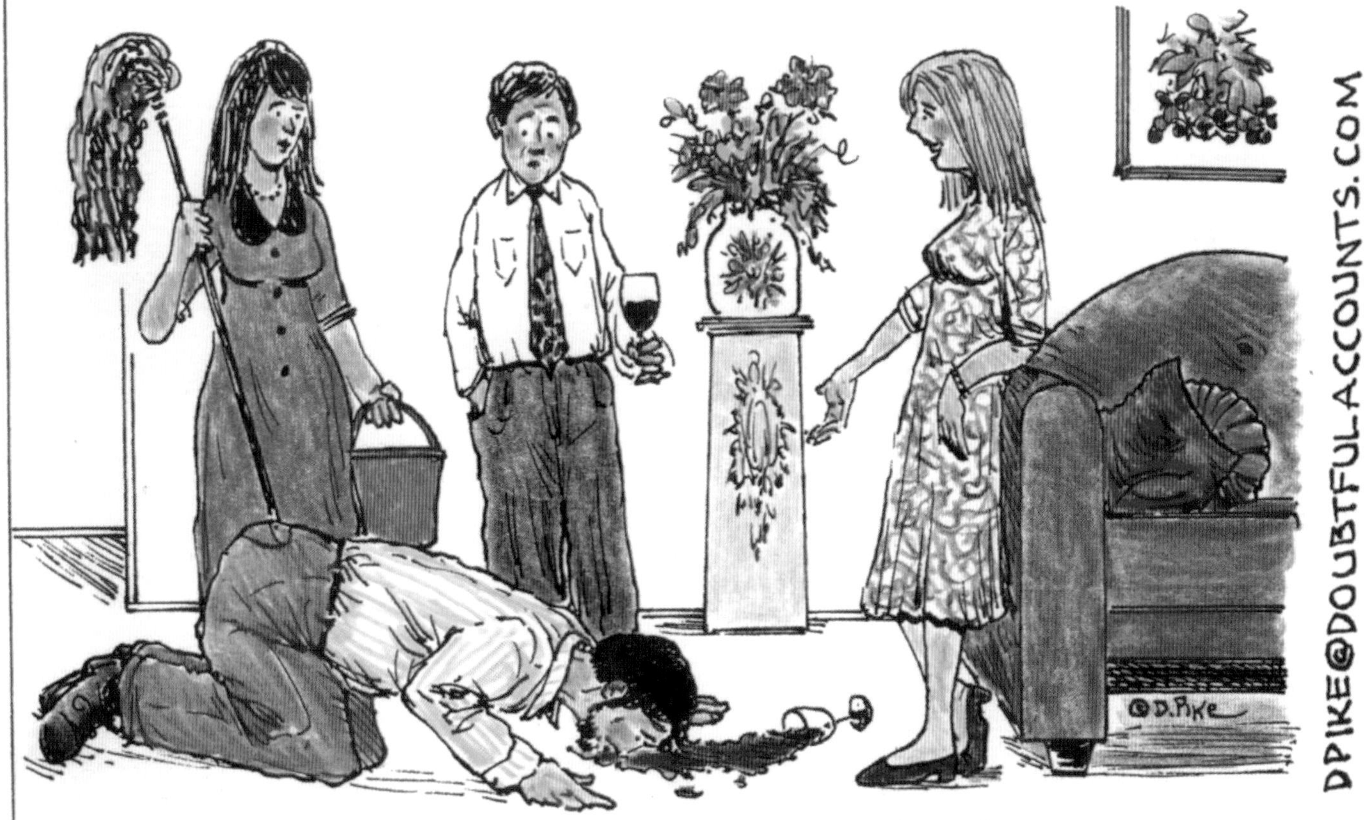
©D.Pike
DPIKE@DOUBTFULACCOUNTS.COM

…and then there's Neal's way of getting a Cotes du Rhone wine stain out of white carpeting.

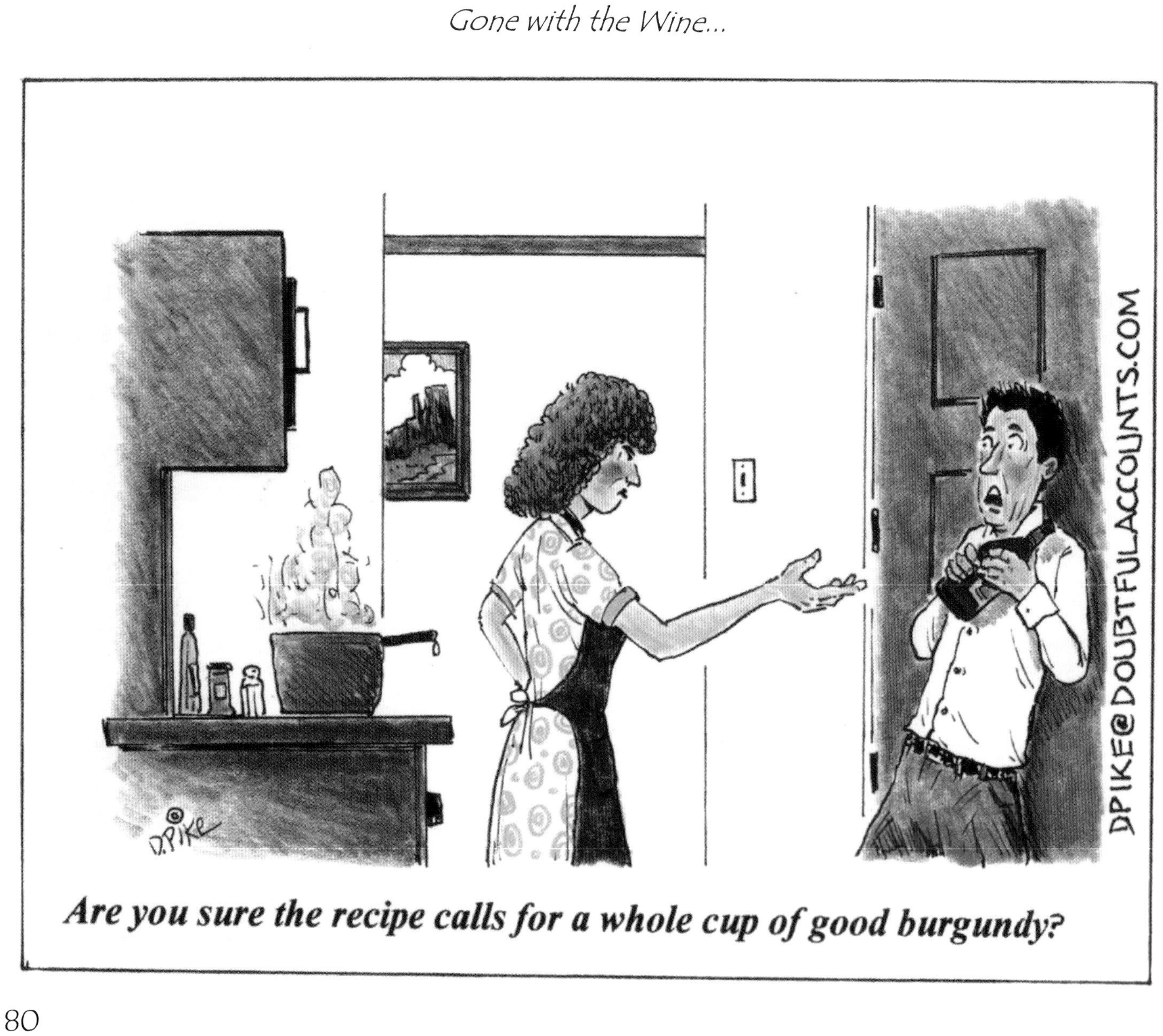
D.PIKE
DPIKE@DOUBTFULACCOUNTS.COM

Are you sure the recipe calls for a whole cup of good burgundy?

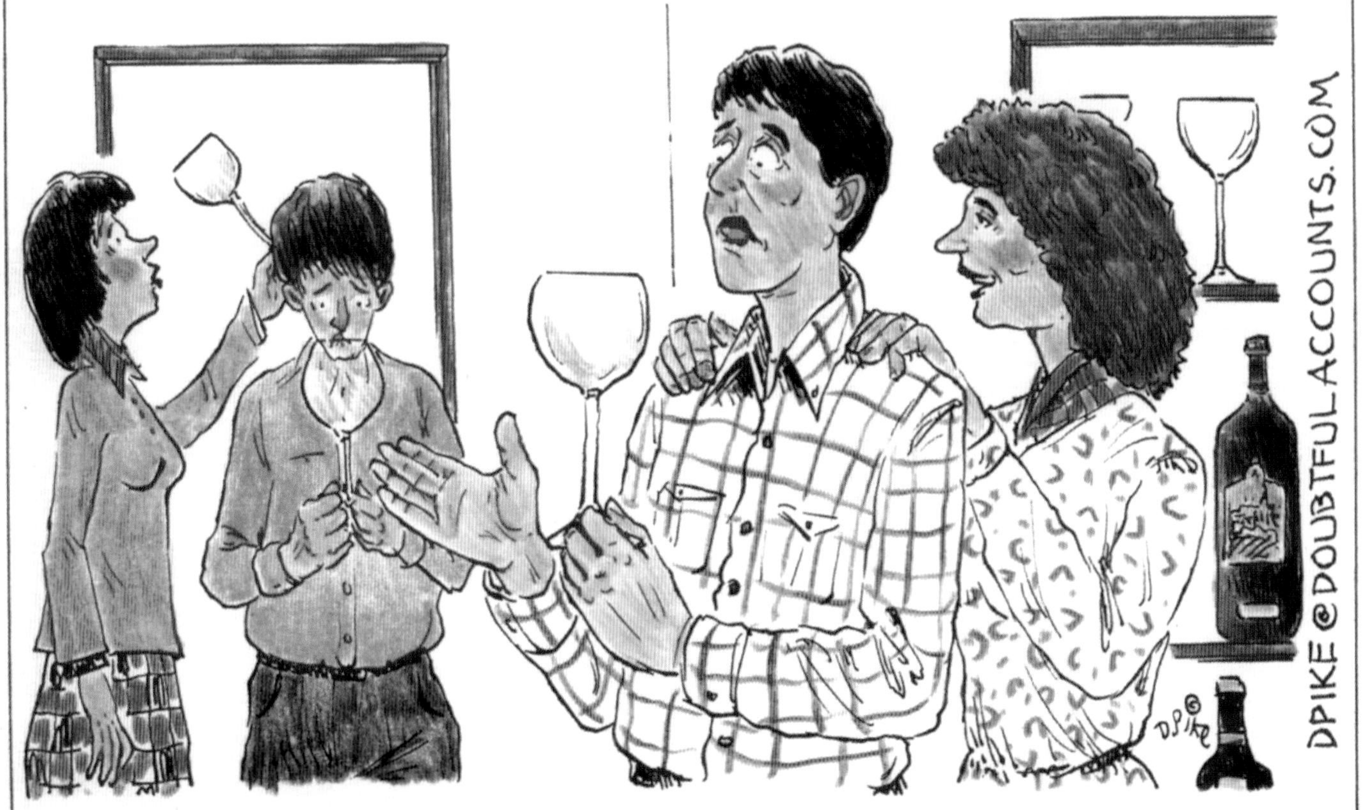
DPIKE@DOUBTFULACCOUNTS.COM
D.Pike©

**You can stop lecturing us about the wine now, Ed—
it evaporated.**

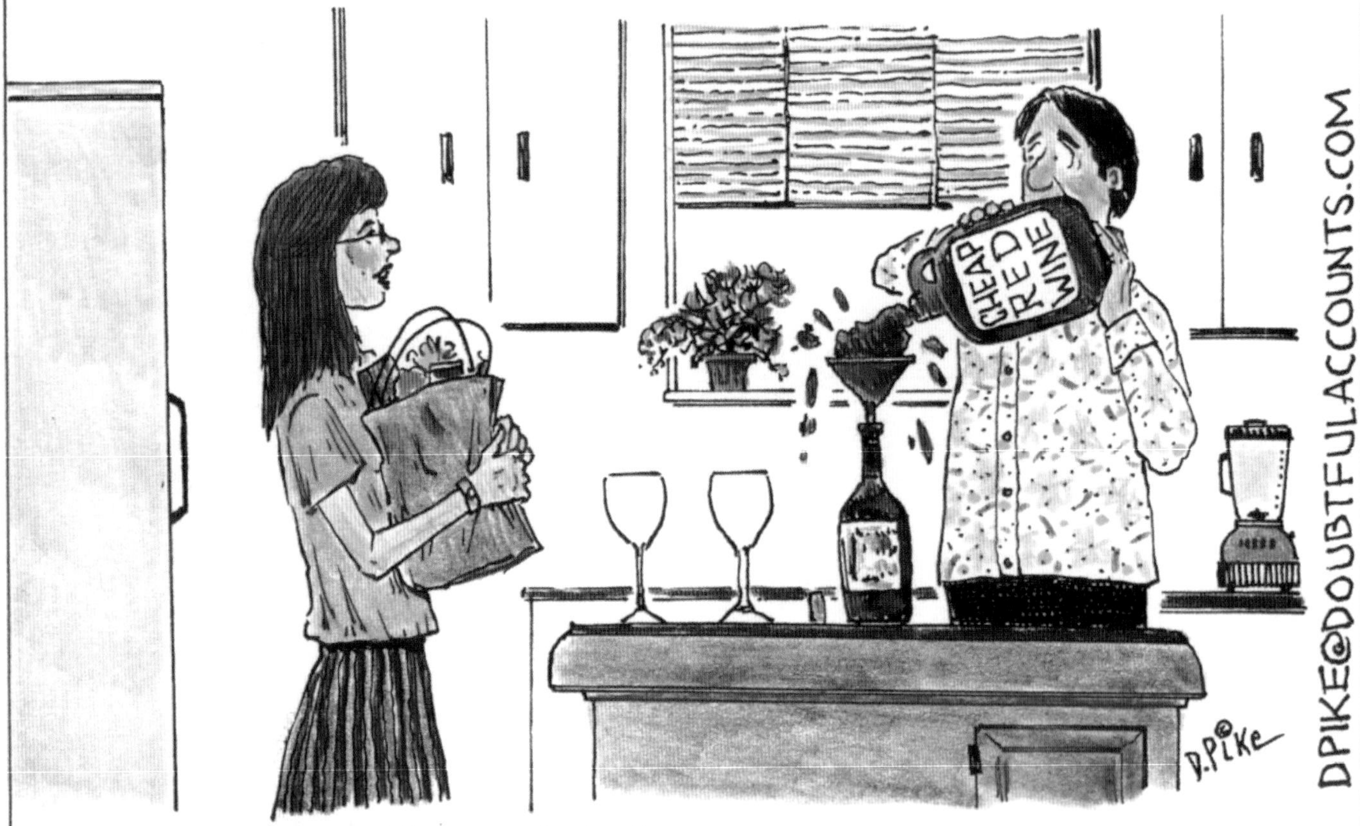
CHEAP
RED
WINE
D.Pike©
DPIKE@DOUBTFULACCOUNTS.COM

***Refilling the '89 Chateau Haut-Brion, I see.
Mind if we get my engagement ring appraised tomorrow?***

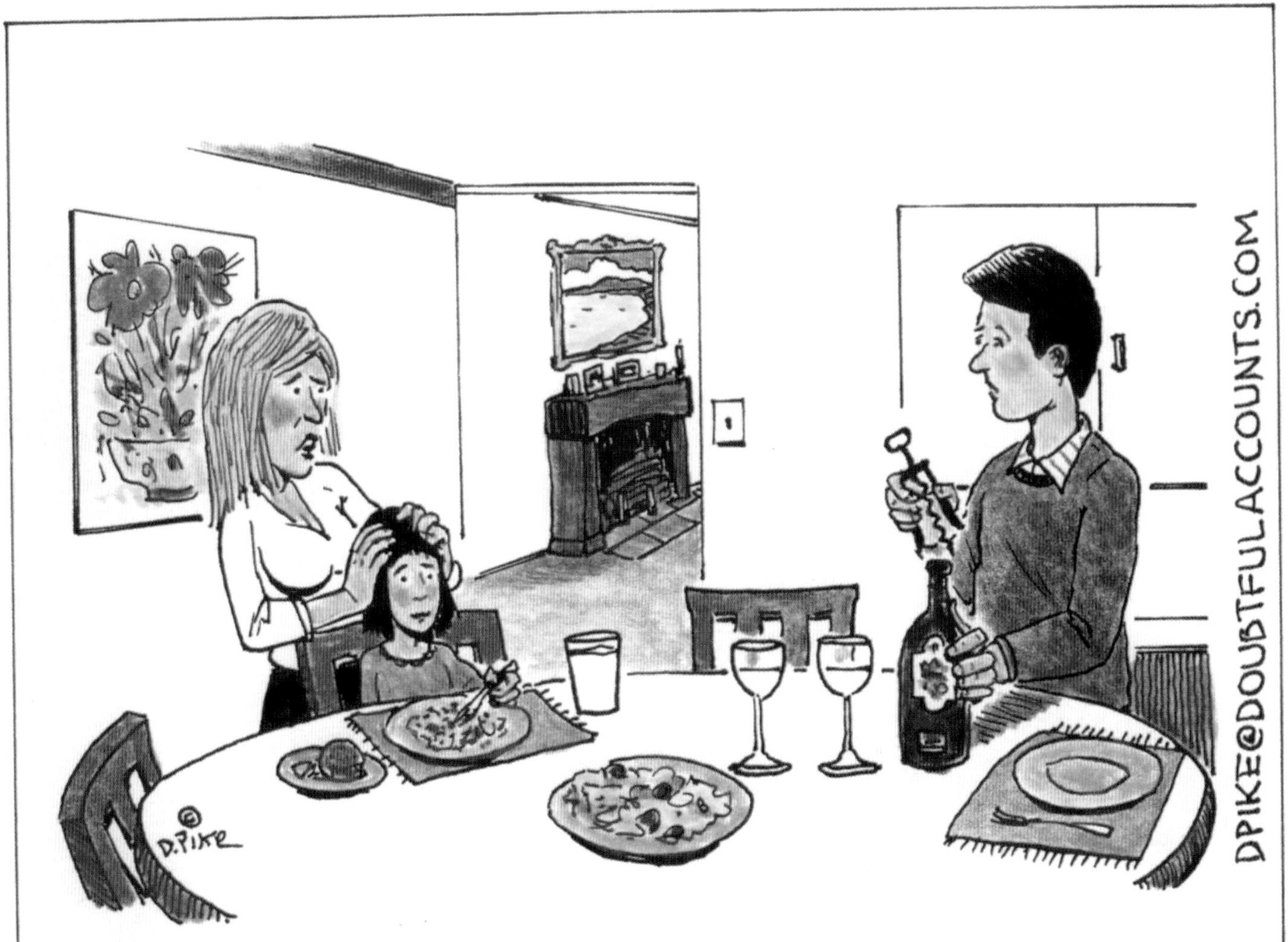
© D.Pike
DPIKE@DOUBTFULACCOUNTS.COM

Must you say screwpull at the table?

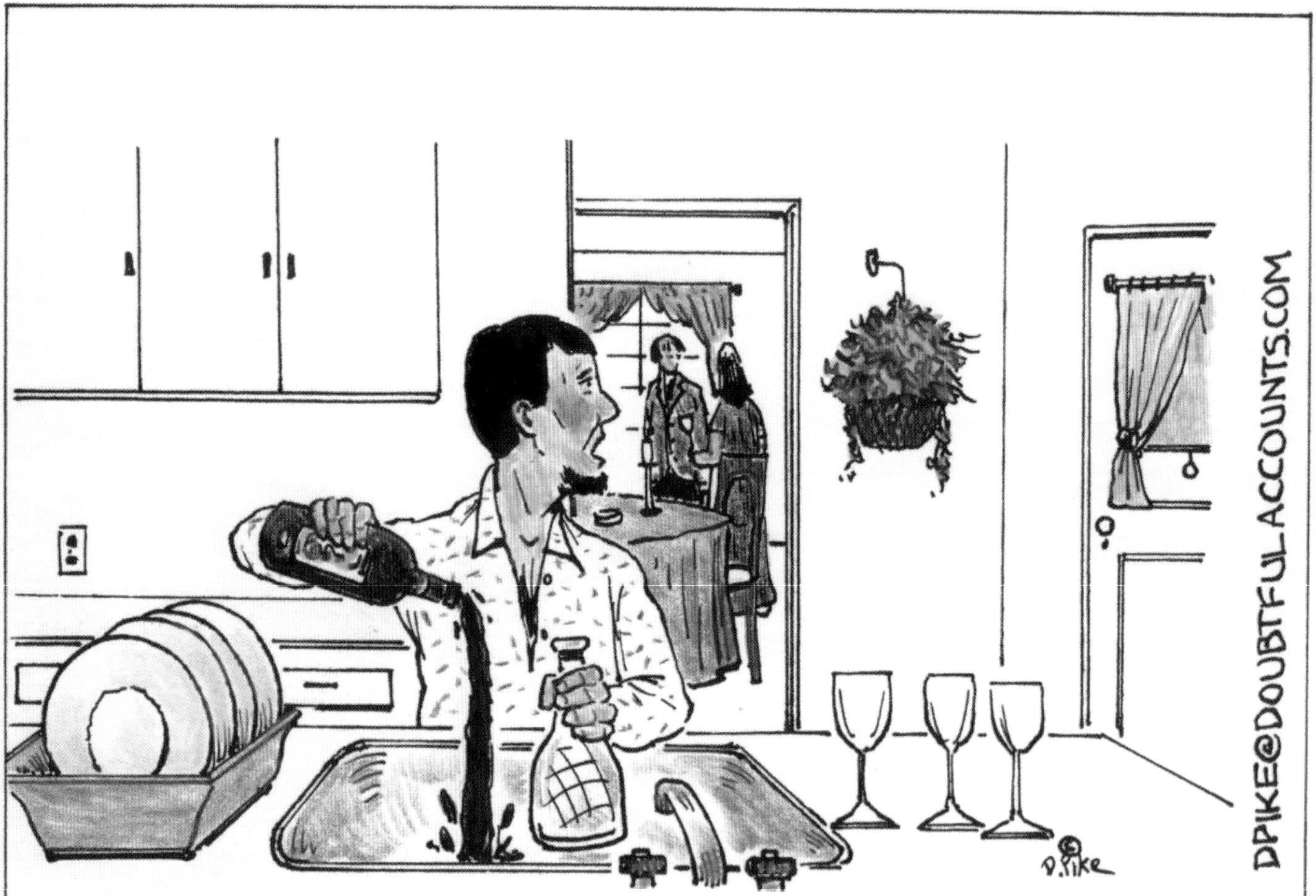
DPIKE@DOUBTFULACCOUNTS.COM

Just decanting the wine, Dear; I'll be in, in a sec. Someone's at the door; and oh, yeah, the dog needs to be let in.

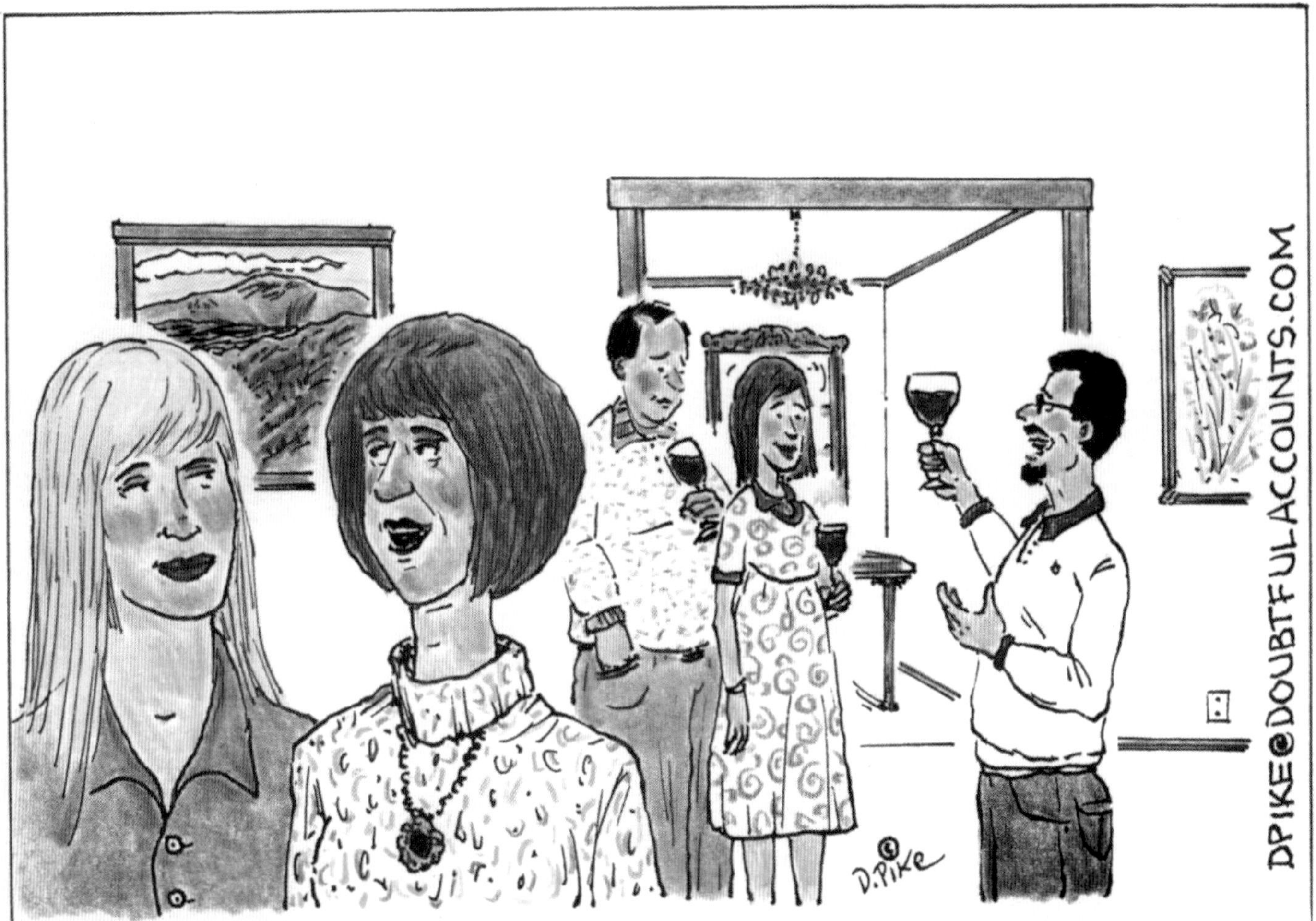
DPIKE@DOUBTFULACCOUNTS.COM
© D.Pike

I've learned a lot from Jack talking about wine. Every time he starts, I go in the other room and find something to read.

6

Lord of the Rieslings: Wine and Life

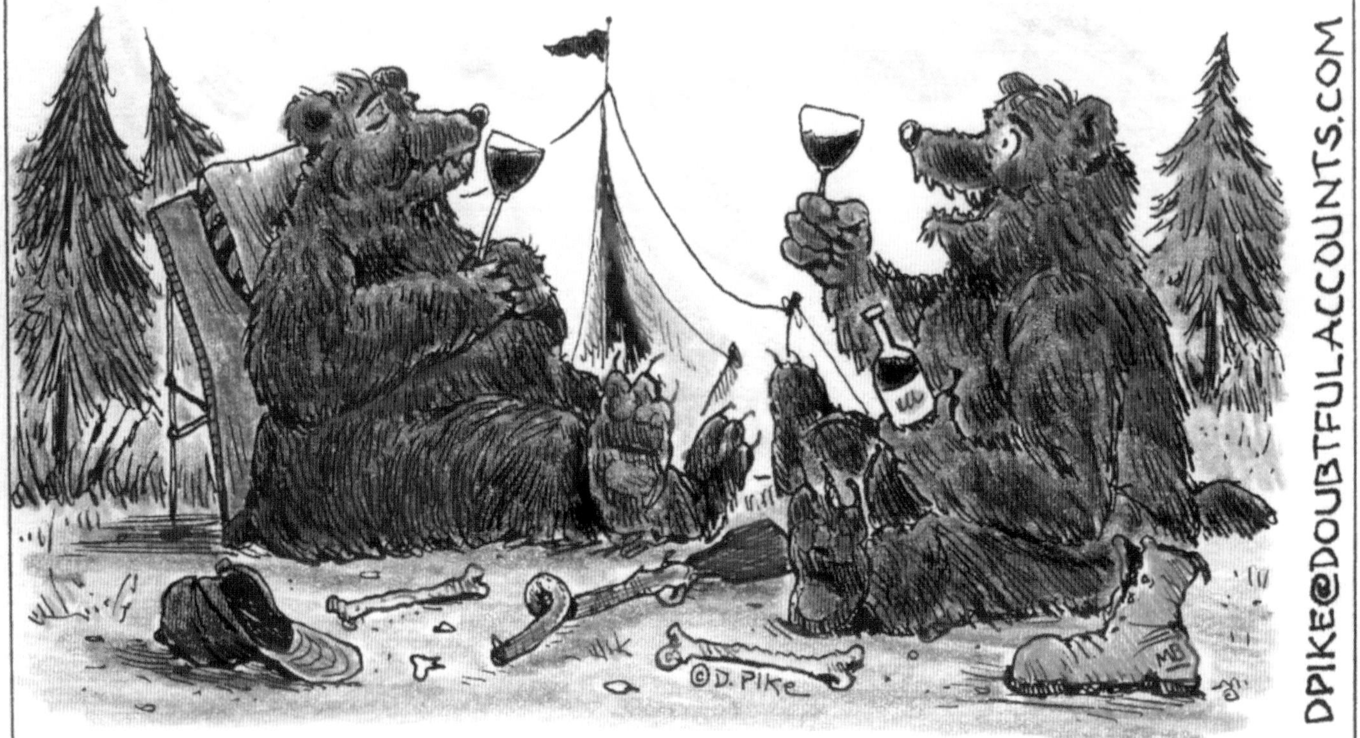
©D. Pike
DPIKE@DOUBTFULACCOUNTS.COM

I finally remembered—red with hunter, white with fisherman.

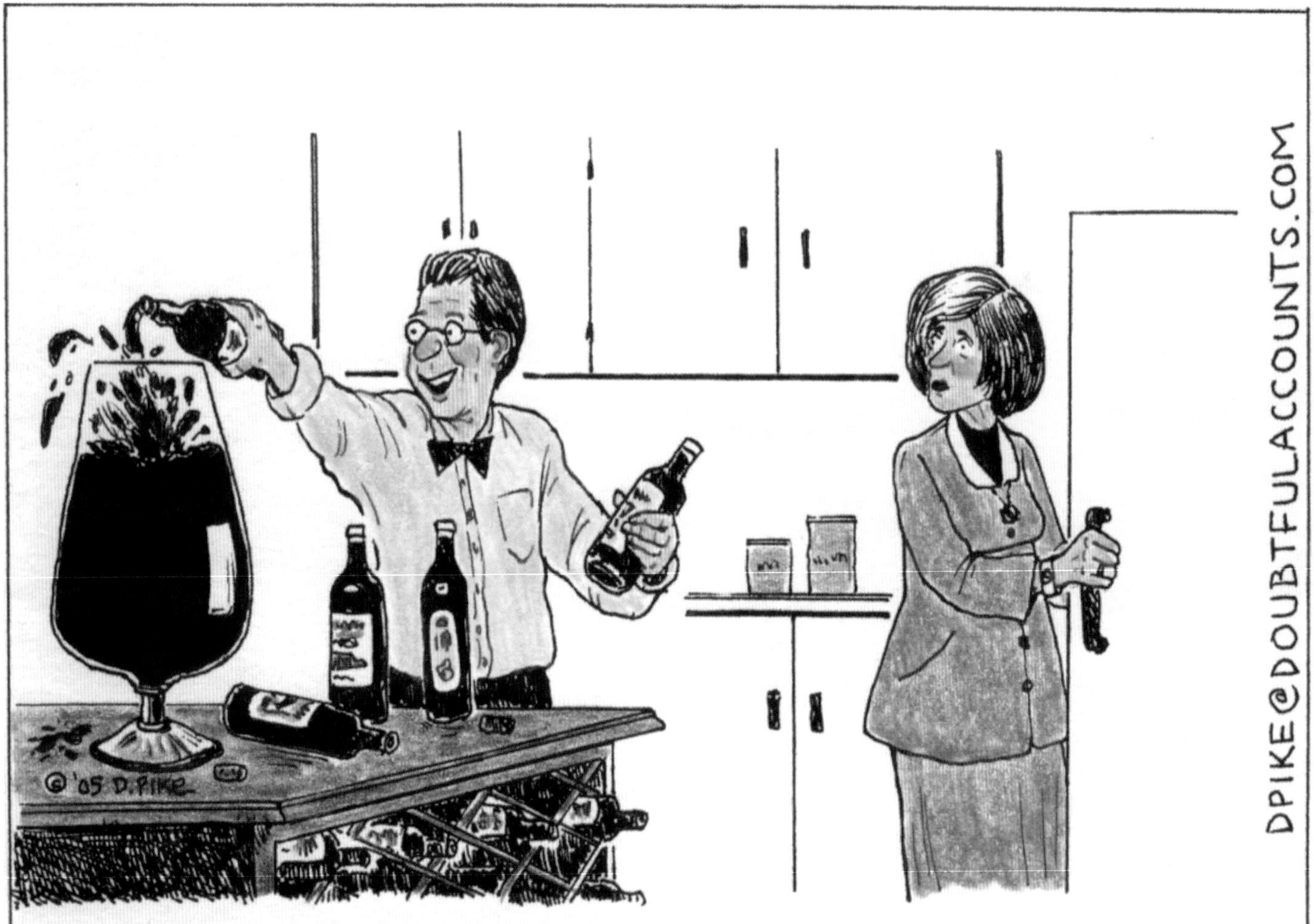
© '05 D. PIKE
DPIKE@DOUBTFULACCOUNTS.COM

I am following orders. Doc said I should limit myself to one glass of wine a day.

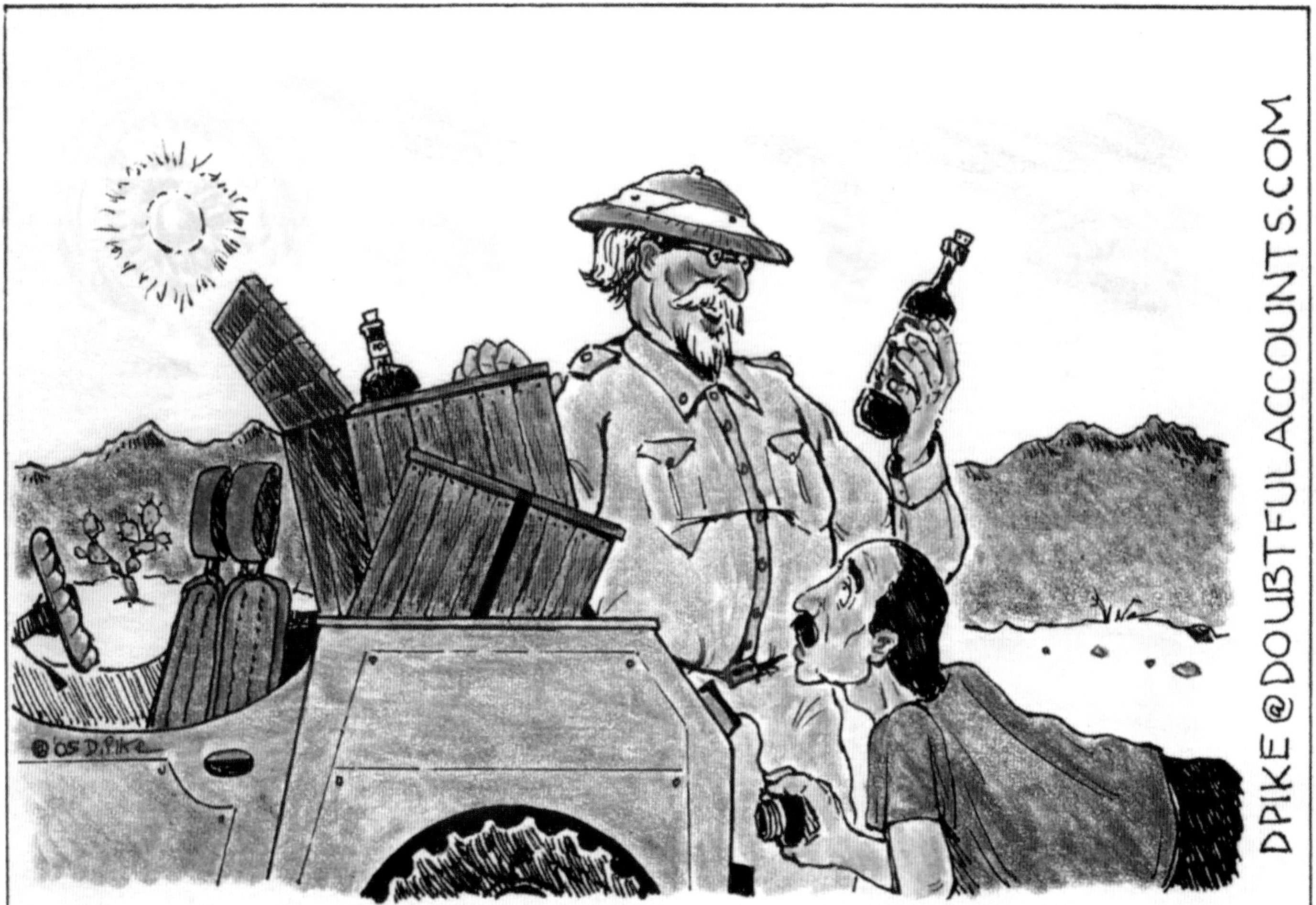
DPIKE@DOUBTFULACCOUNTS.COM
© '05 D. Pike

Out of petrol? Not a problem—we'll fill her up with Trendy Vineyards' 40-proof Cabernet Sauvignon!

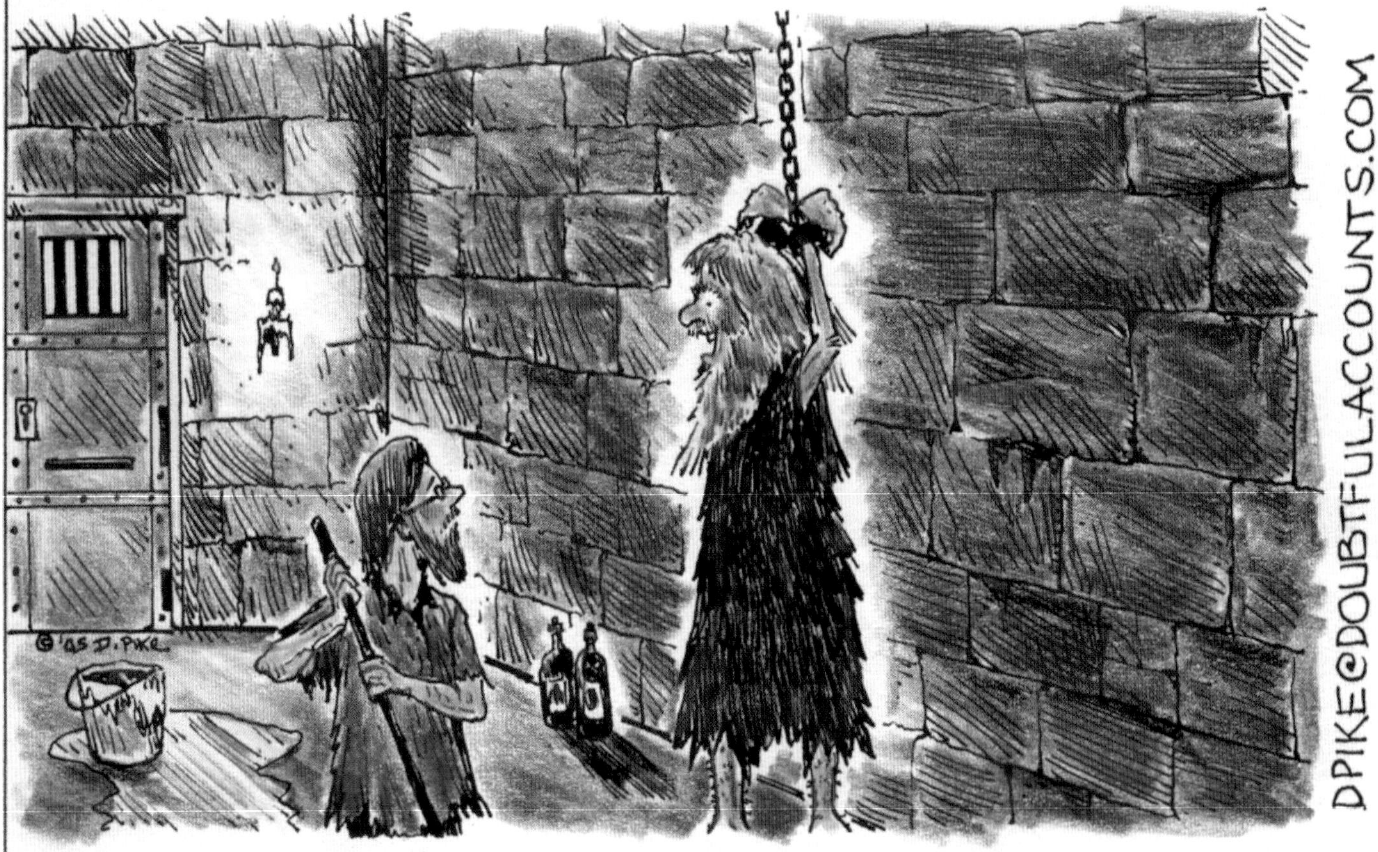
©'05 D. PIKE
DPIKE@DOUBTFULACCOUNTS.COM

It's cold, damp and dark, but I can't complain—
it's perfect for my clarets.

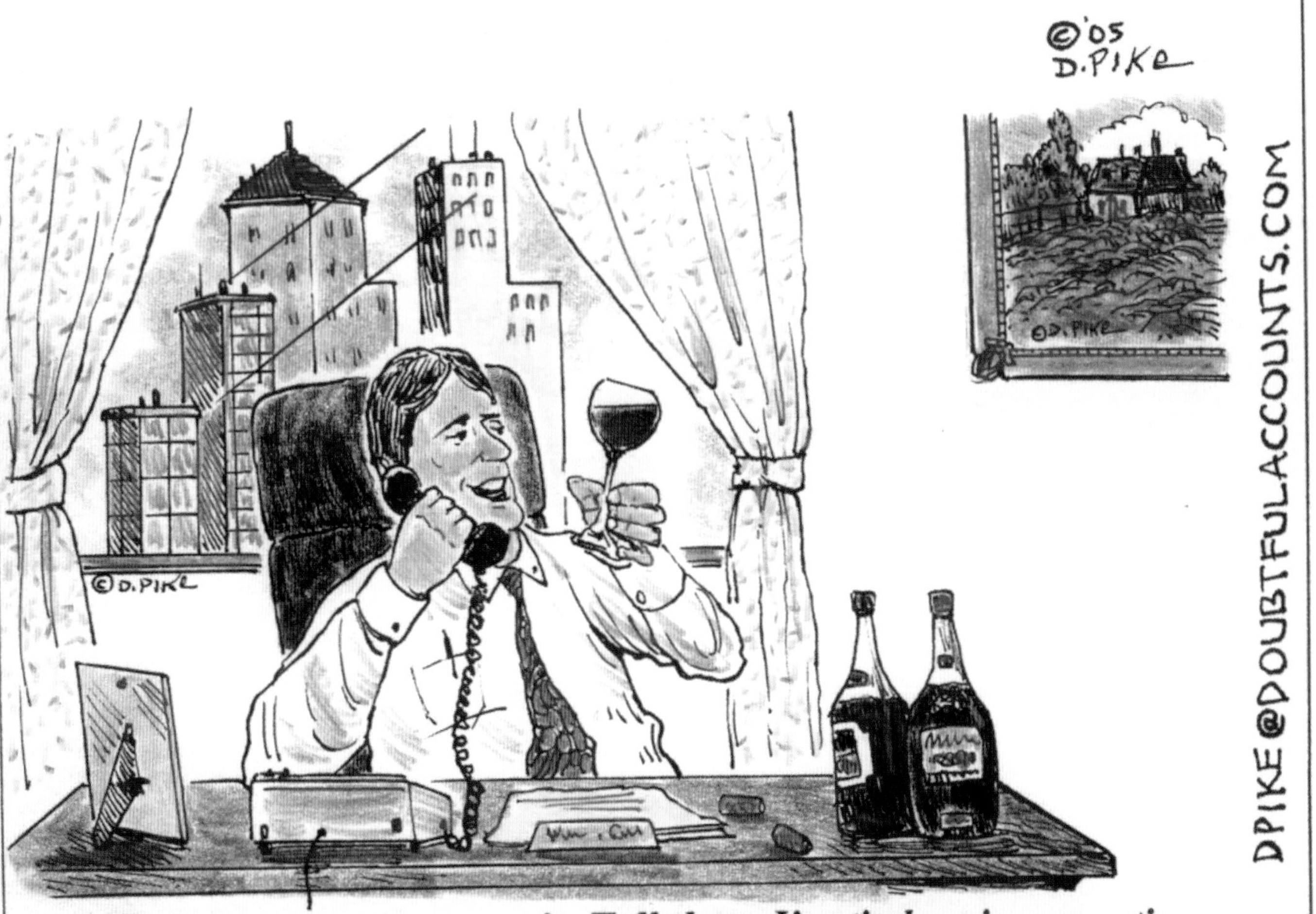
©'05
D.PIKE
©D.PIKE
©D.PIKE
DPIKE@DOUBTFULACCOUNTS.COM

The accountants can wait. Tell them I'm tied up in a meeting with representatives from Pomerol & Pommard.

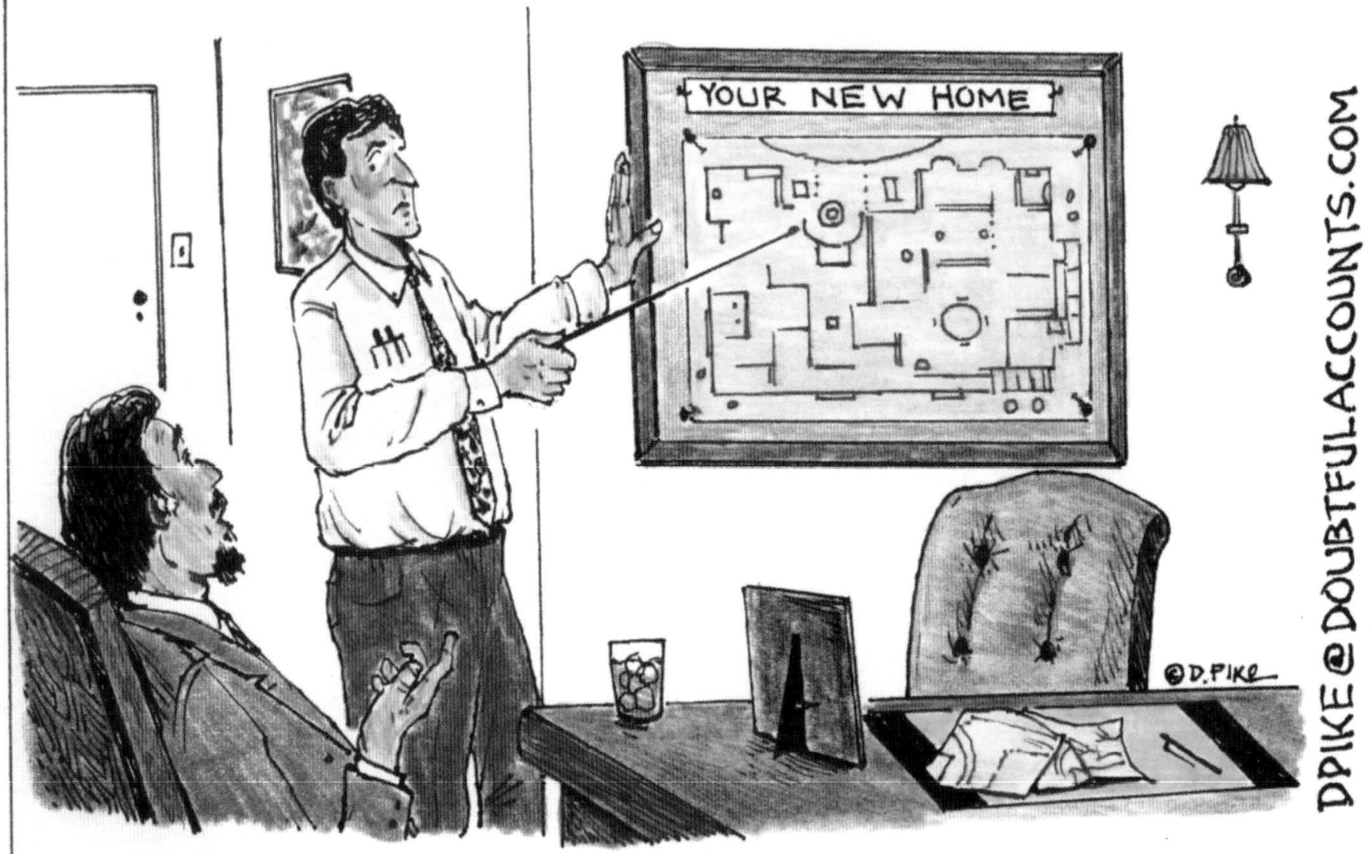
YOUR NEW HOME
©D.PIKE
DPIKE@DOUBTFULACCOUNTS.COM

Who needs central heating? I've got plenty of vintage port.

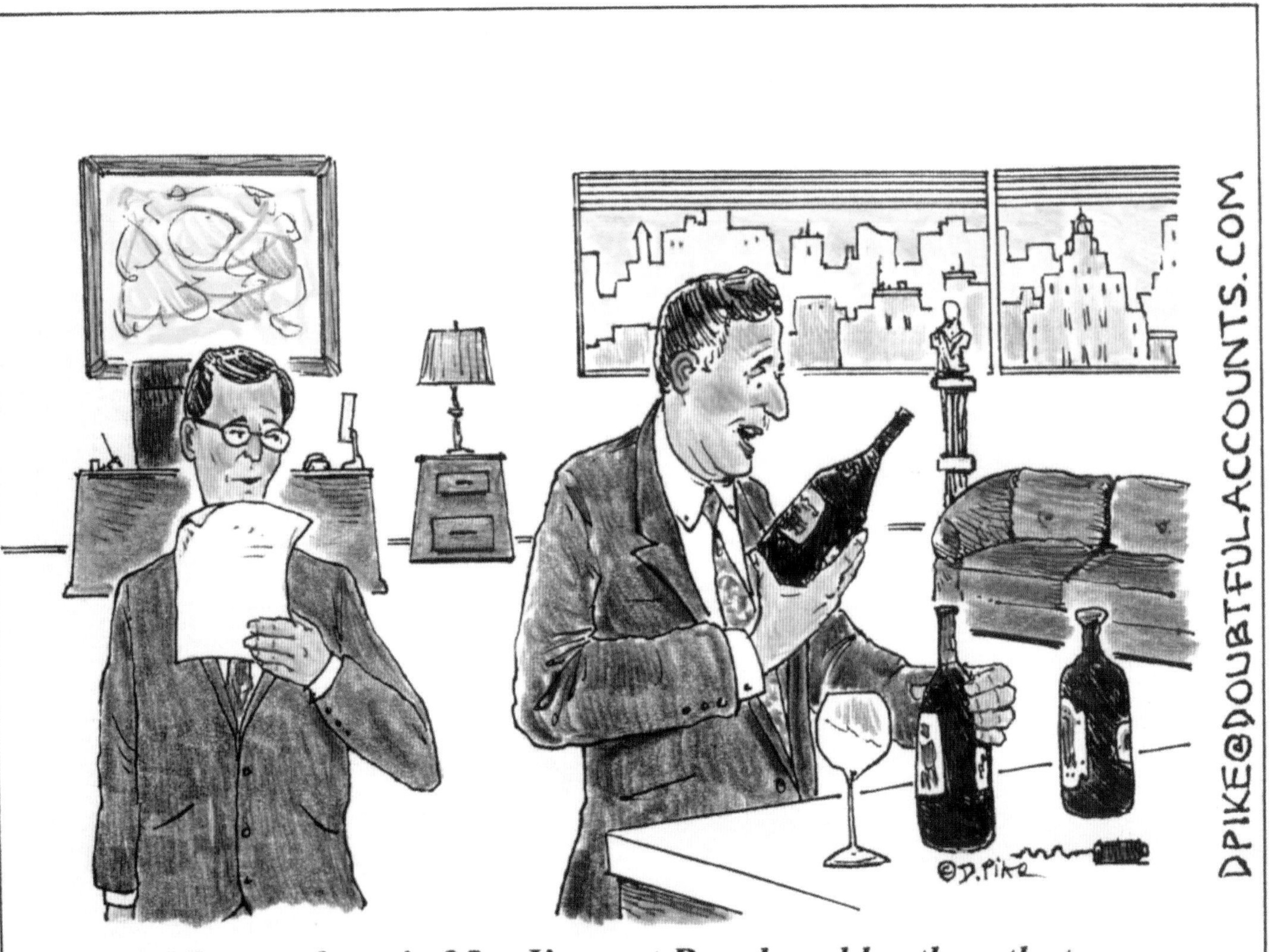
DPIKE@DOUBTFULACCOUNTS.COM
©D.PIKE

My new boss is 25—I've got Barolos older than that.

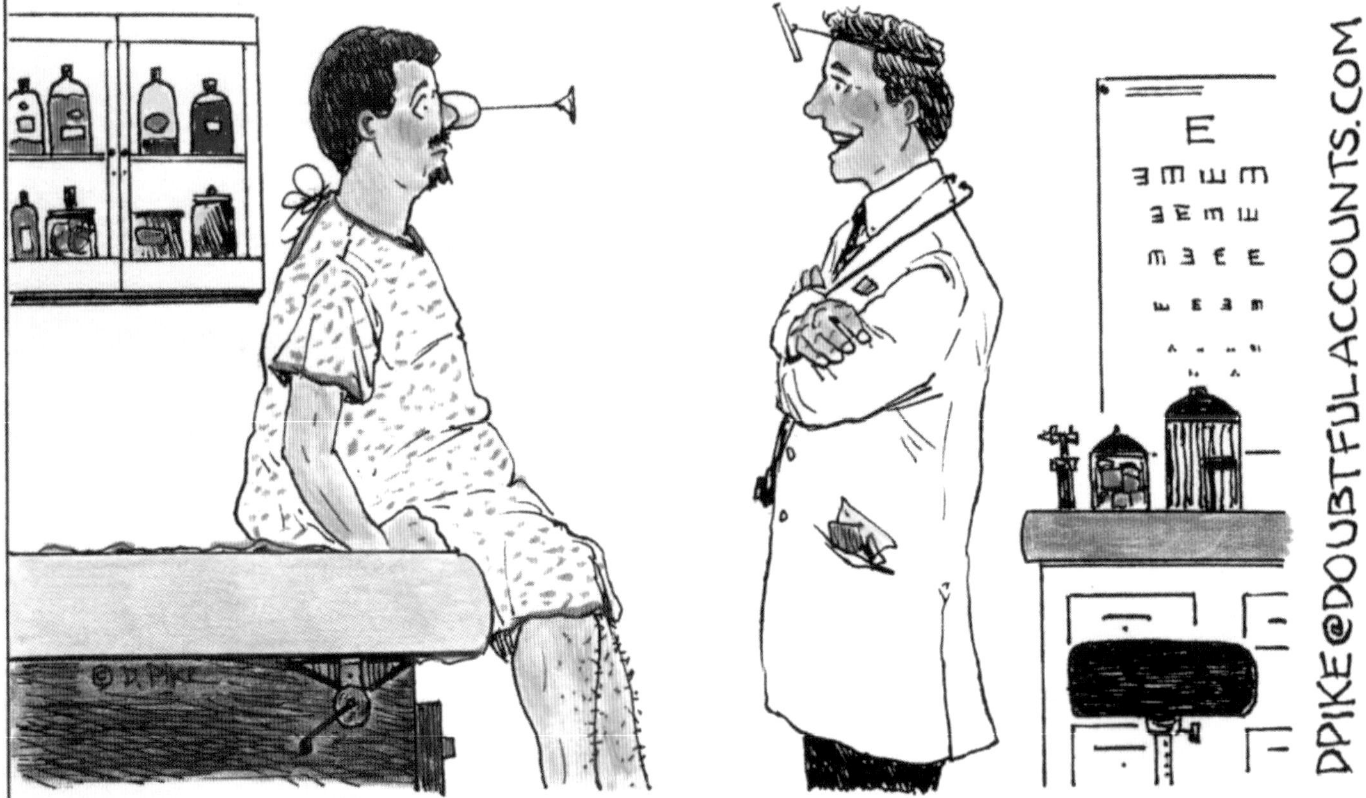
DPIKE@DOUBTFULACCOUNTS.COM

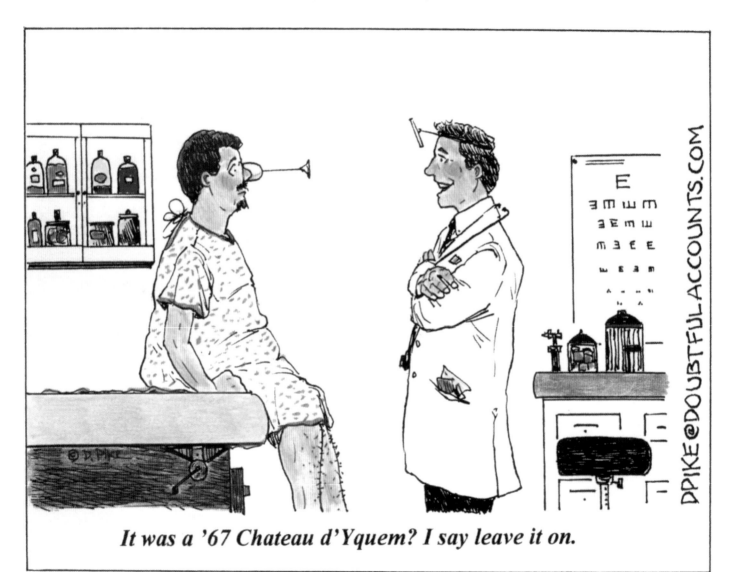

It was a '67 Chateau d'Yquem? I say leave it on.

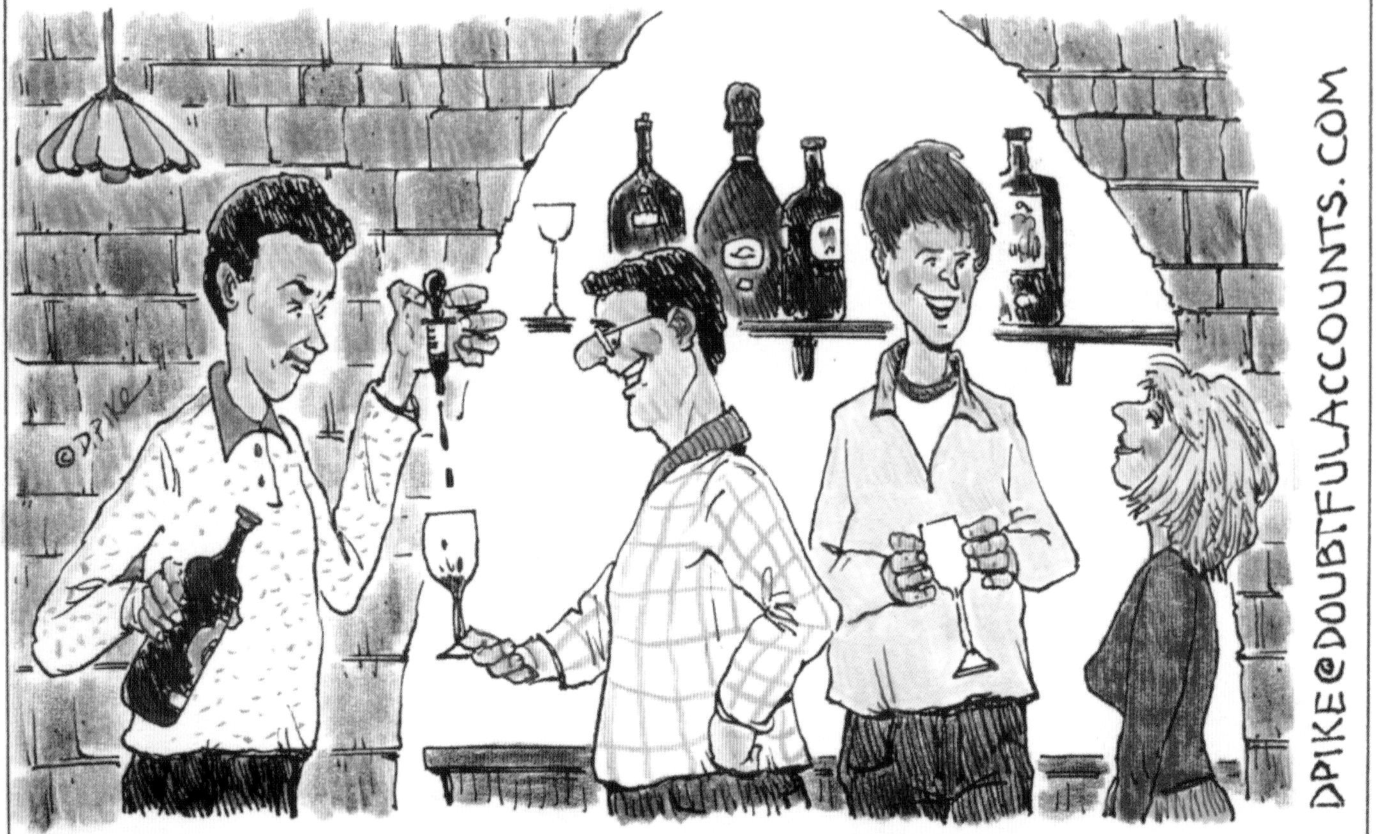
DPIKE@DOUBTFULACCOUNTS.COM

I see Kevin is being unusually generous with his Chateau Margaux this evening.

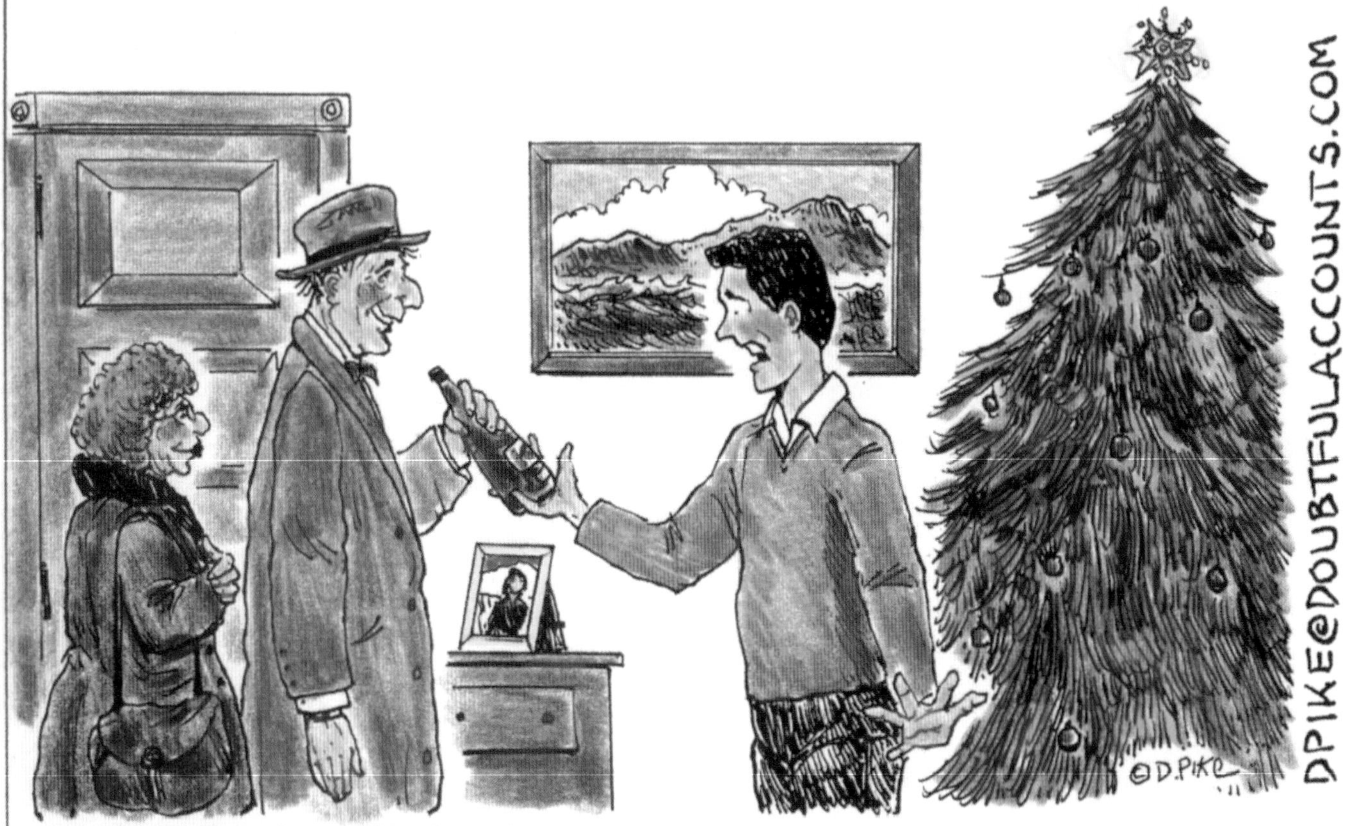
©D.PIKE
DPIKE@DOUBTFULACCOUNTS.COM

A 1982 bottle of KMart Beaujolais Nouveau? You shouldn't have, really. I mean you really, really shouldn't have...really.

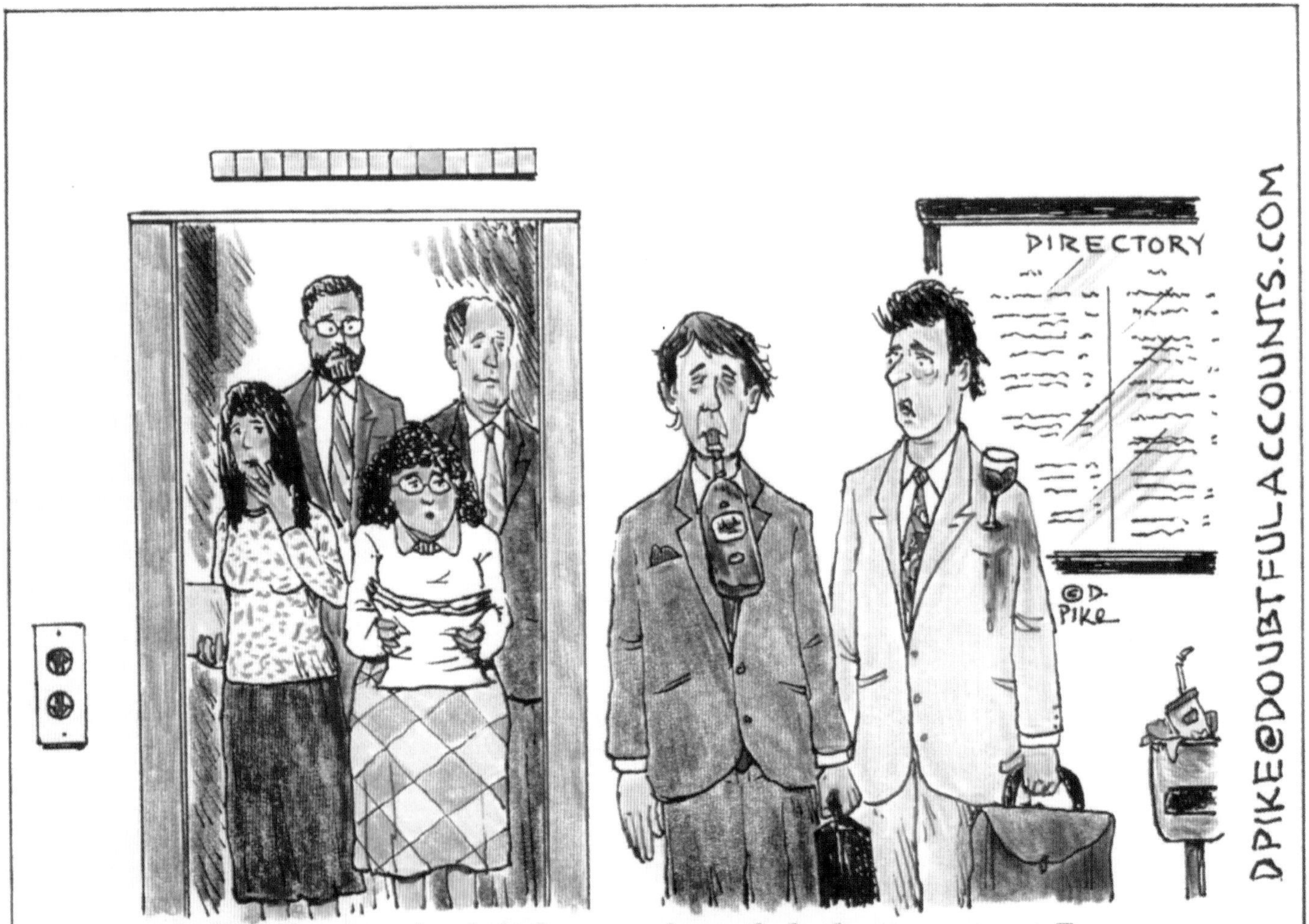
DIRECTORY
©D. PIKE
DPIKE@DOUBTFULACCOUNTS.COM

I dunno, maybe joining a wine club that meets at 7 a.m. on Monday mornings wasn't such a good idea after all.

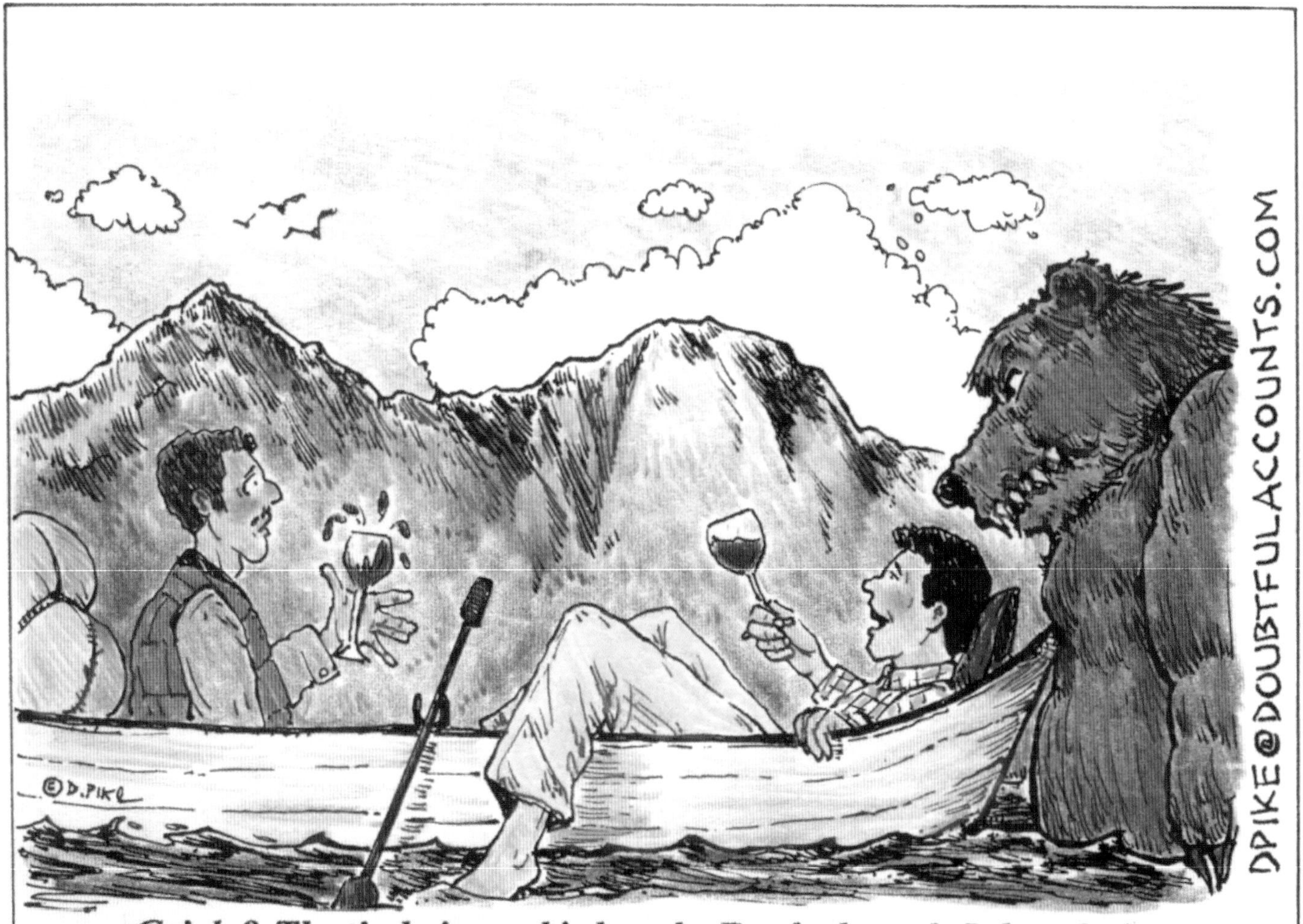
©D.PIKE
DPIKE@DOUBTFULACCOUNTS.COM

Grisly? That's being a bit harsh, Paul, though I do admit it's a bit rough around the edges.

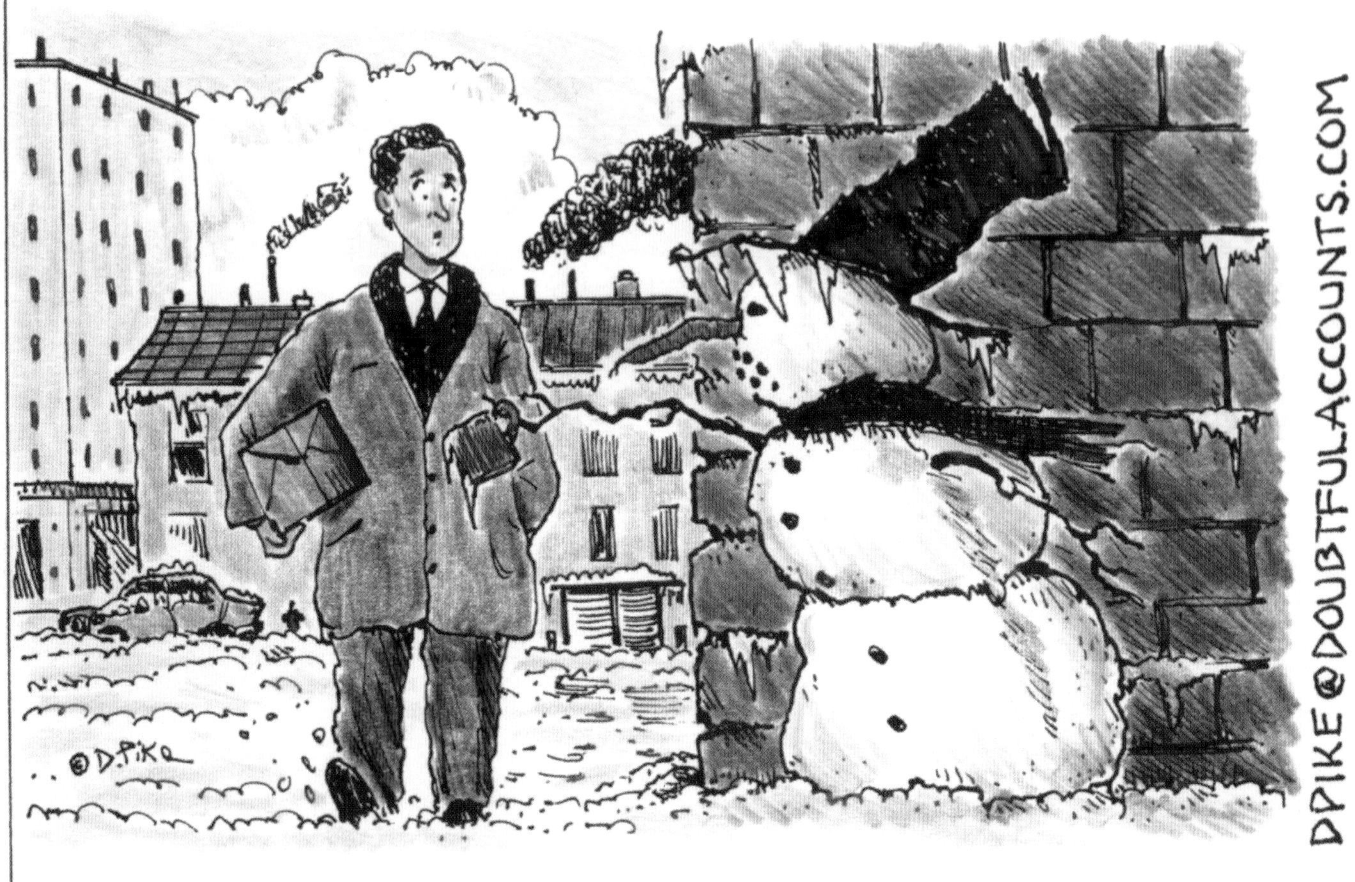
©D.Pike
DPIKE@DOUBTFULACCOUNTS.COM

Hey buddy; can you spare a couple of bucks for a glass of eiswein?

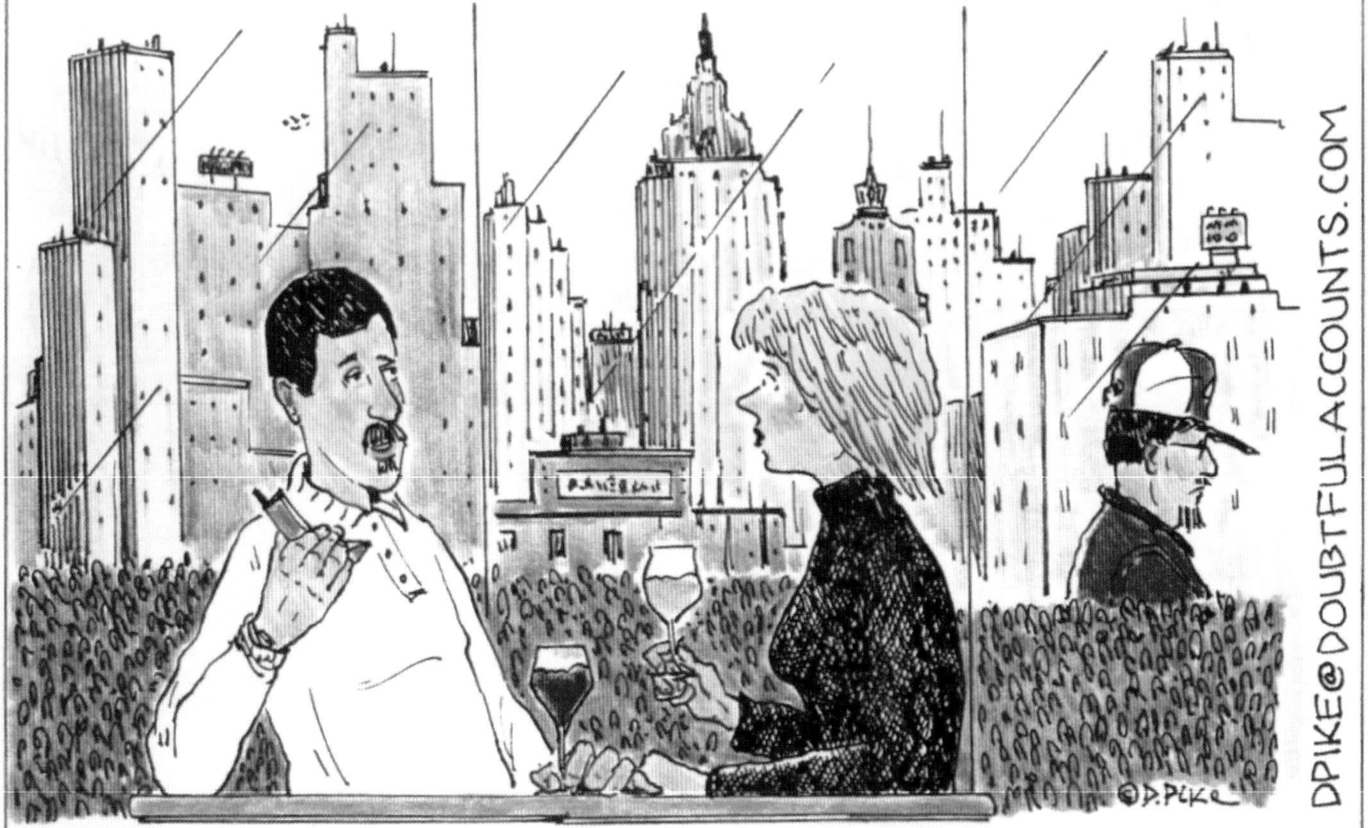
©D.PIKE
DPIKE@DOUBTFULACCOUNTS.COM

The travel agent says there's nothing available on the port side. Do you want me to see if she's got anything on the sherry side?

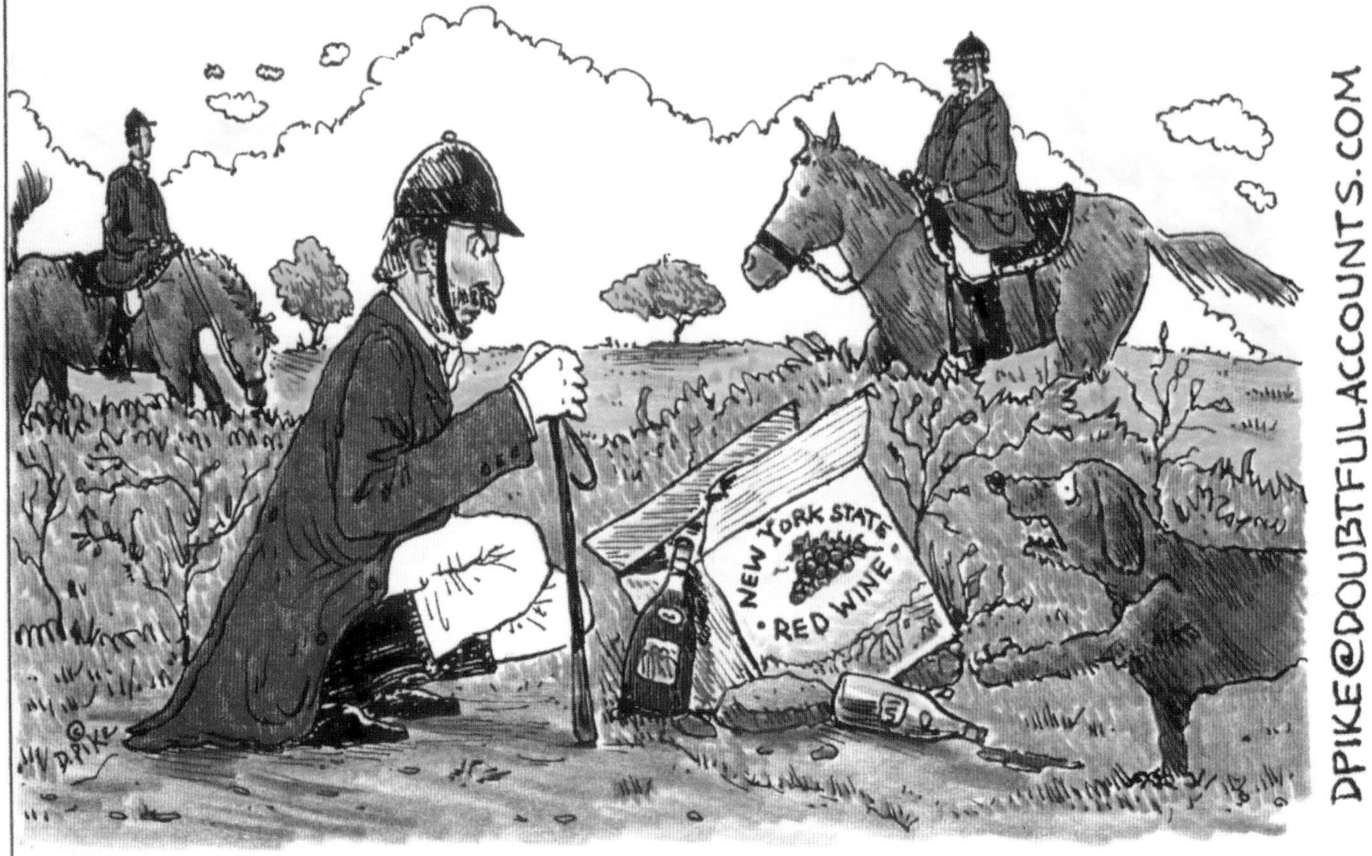
NEW YORK STATE
RED WINE
DPIKE@DOUBTFULACCOUNTS.COM
© D. PIKE

Hey, I'm sorry, it smelled foxy.

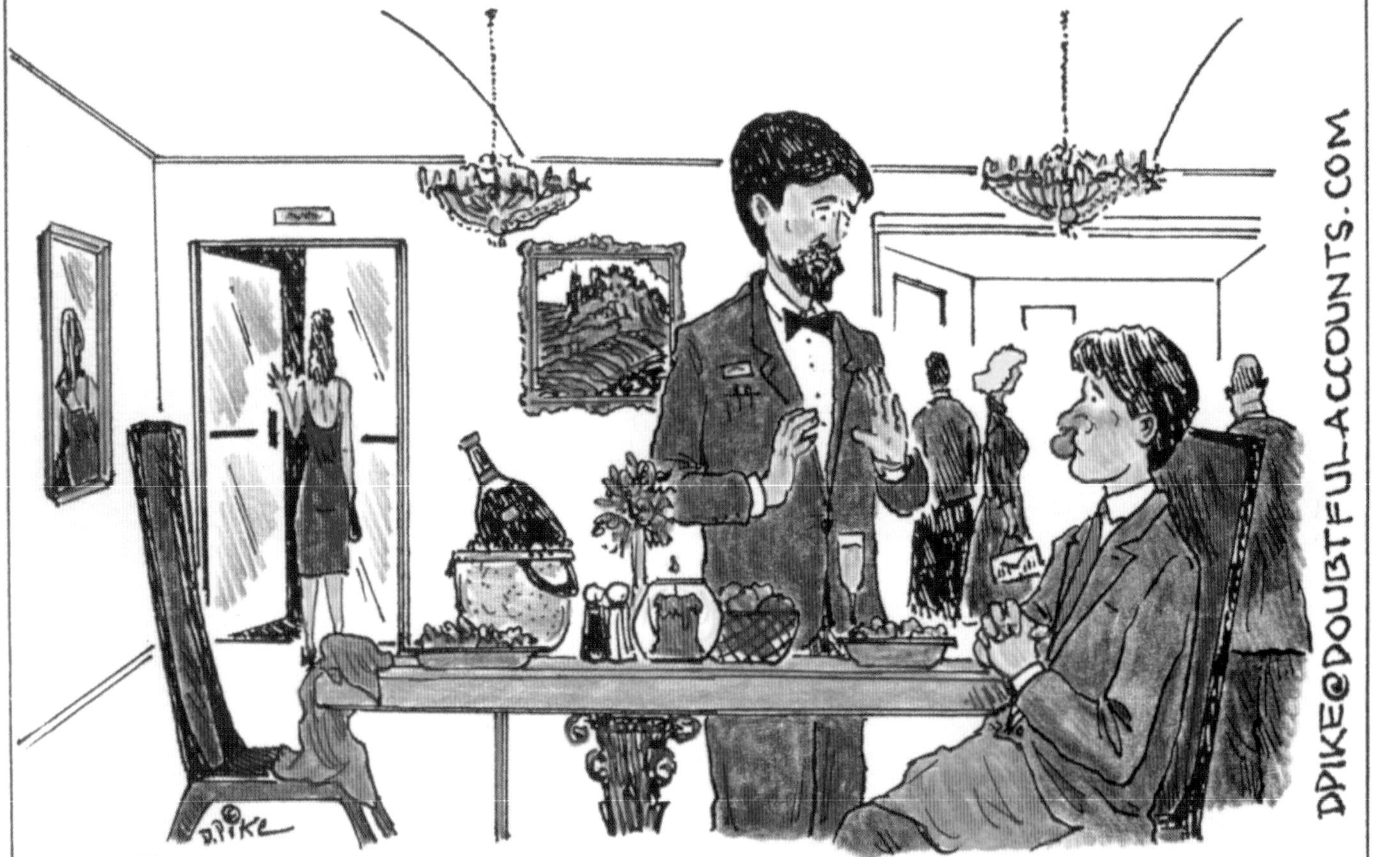
DPIKE@DOUBTFULACCOUNTS.COM

How many times did you think you could get away with using the term "bouchon d'expedition" on the first date?

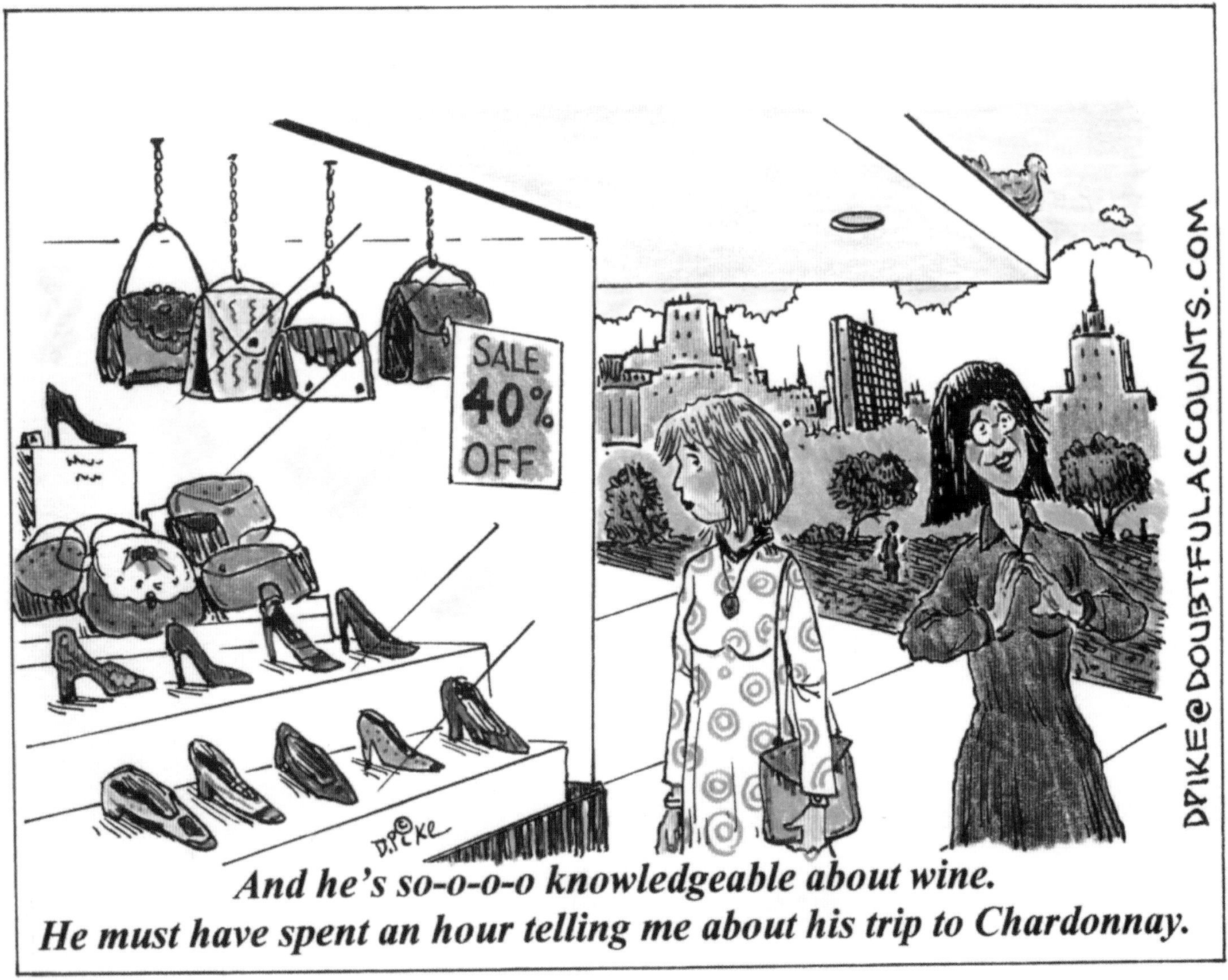
SALE
40%
OFF
DPIKE@DOUBTFULACCOUNTS.COM

And he's so-o-o-o knowledgeable about wine.
He must have spent an hour telling me about his trip to Chardonnay.

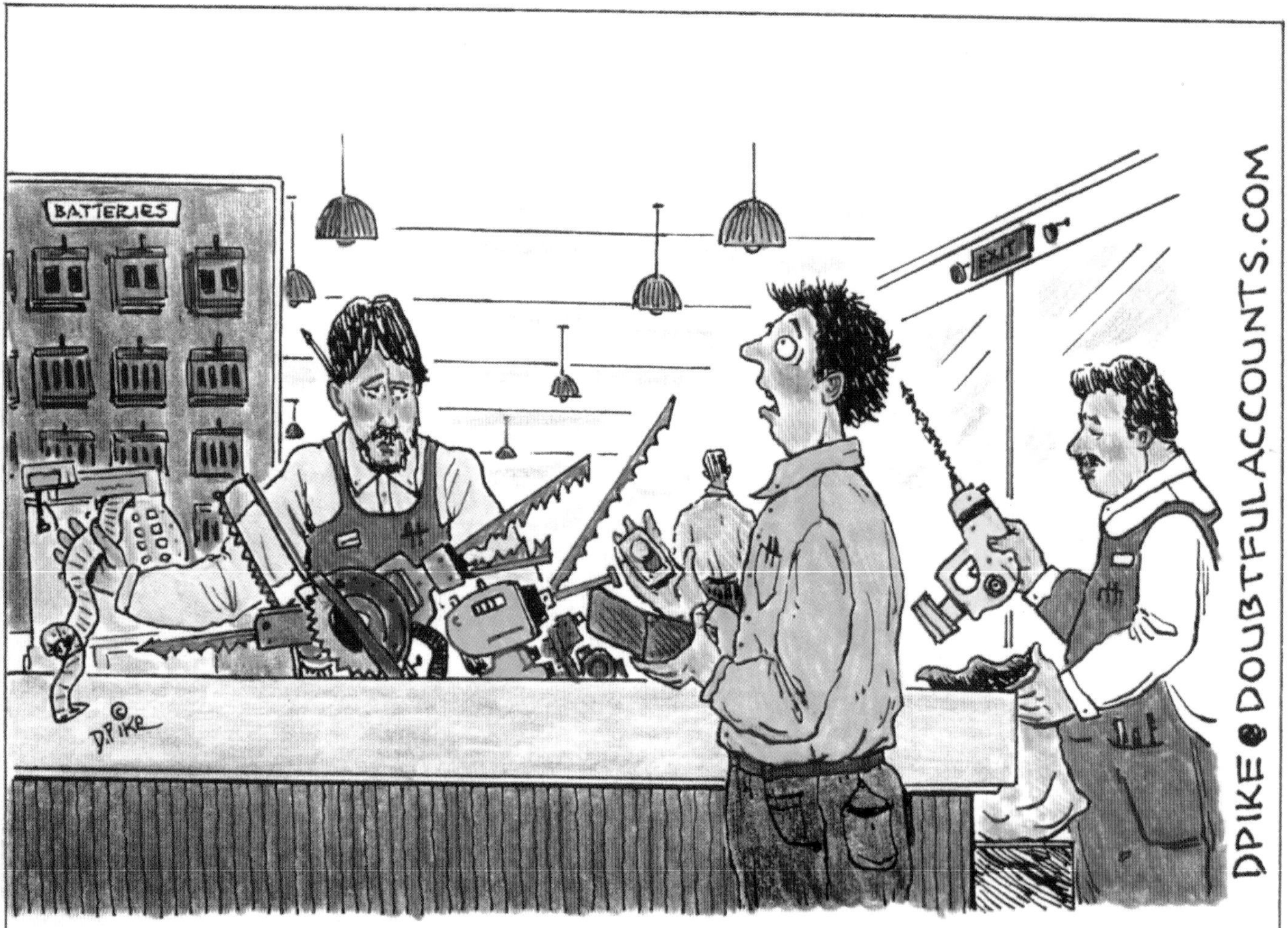
BATTERIES
EXIT
D.PIKE
DPIKE@DOUBTFULACCOUNTS.COM

What home project? I just want to get a wine label off.

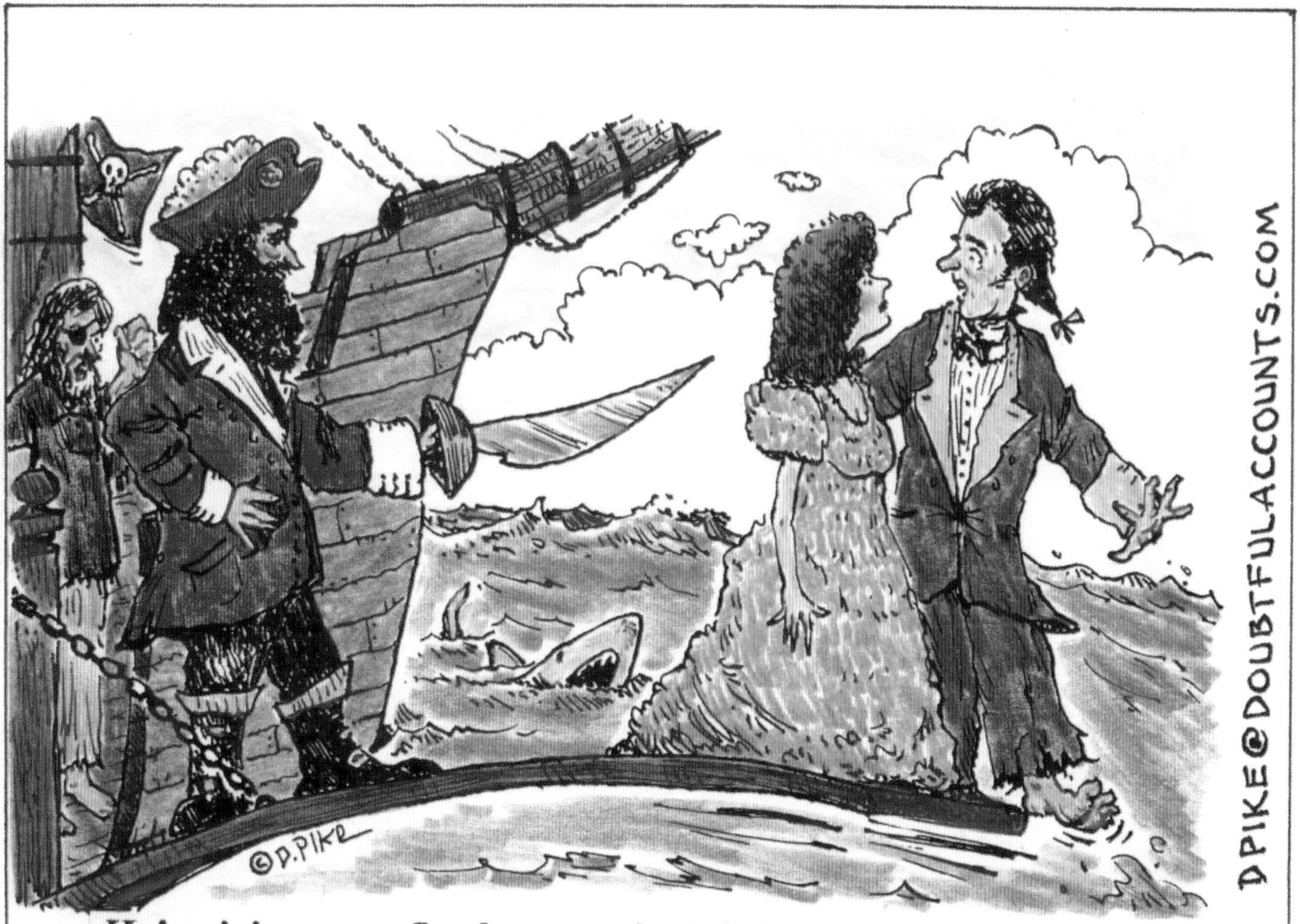
©D.PIKE
DPIKE@DOUBTFULACCOUNTS.COM

He's giving us a final request? Ask for a glass of Beaujolais Nouveau—that'll give us till November.

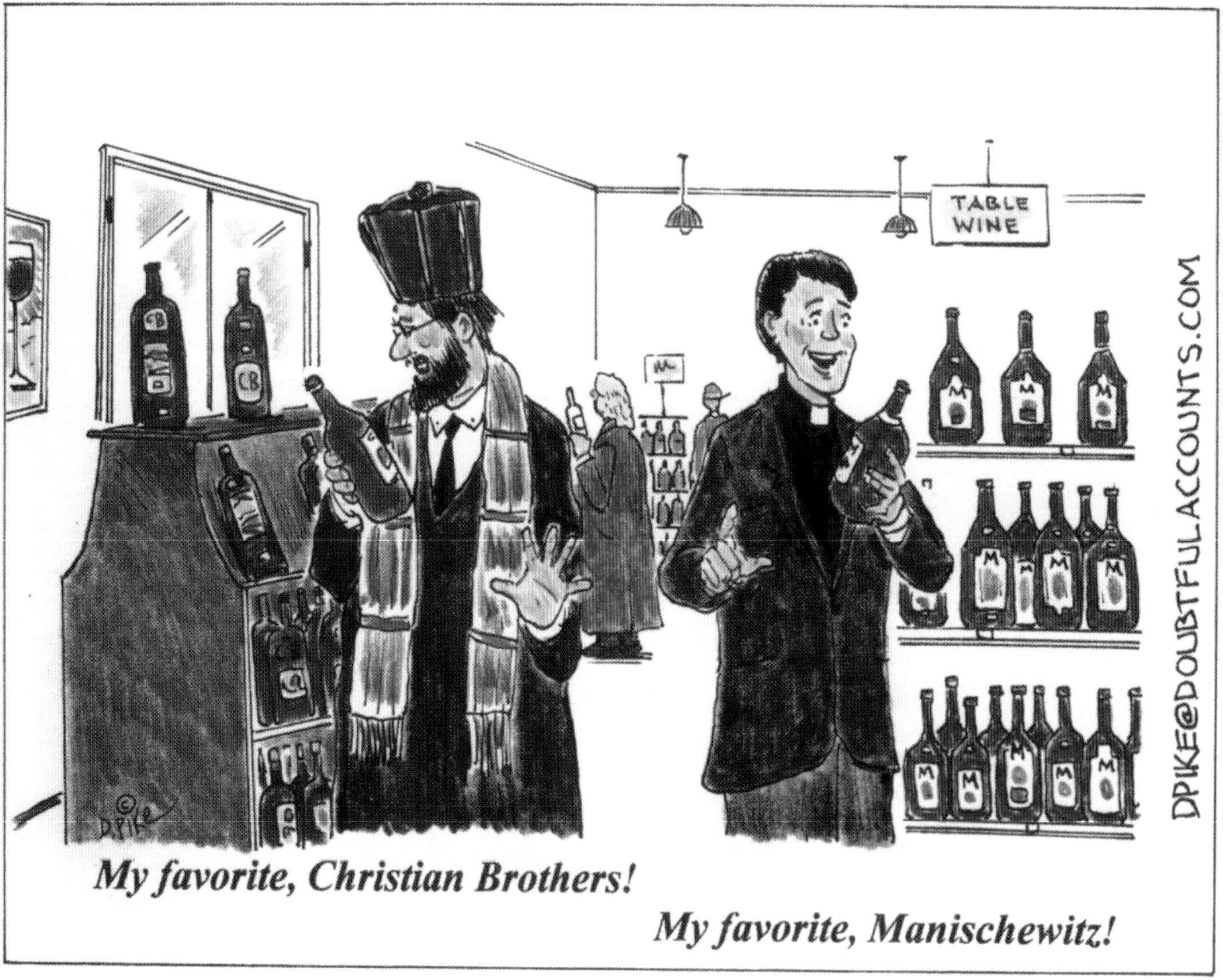
TABLE
WINE
DPIKE@DOUBTFULACCOUNTS.COM

My favorite, Christian Brothers!

My favorite, Manischewitz!

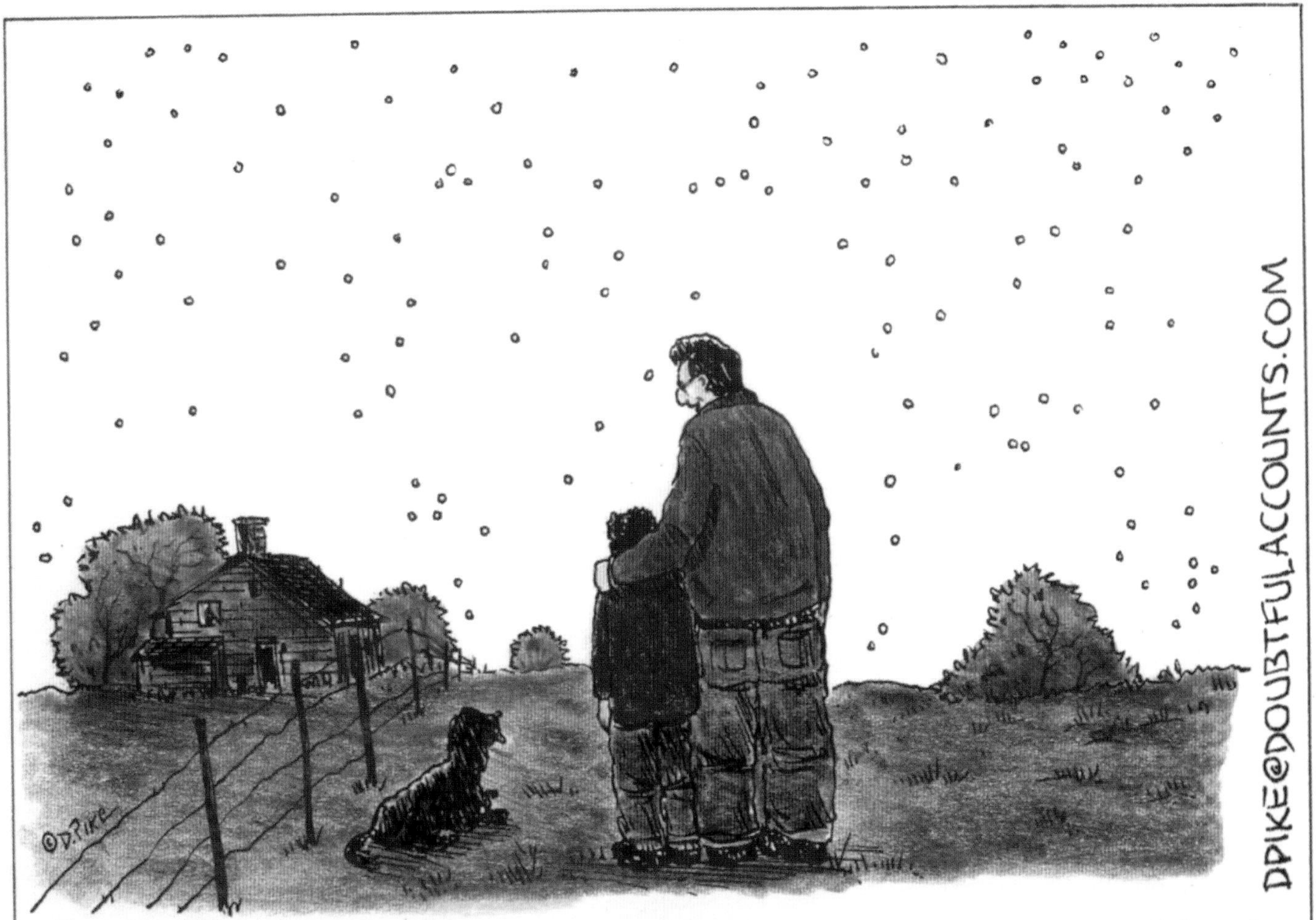
©D.PIKE
DPIKE@DOUBTFULACCOUNTS.COM

Yes, there are a lot of stars, Son. Not as many as there are California Chardonnays, but a lot, just the same.

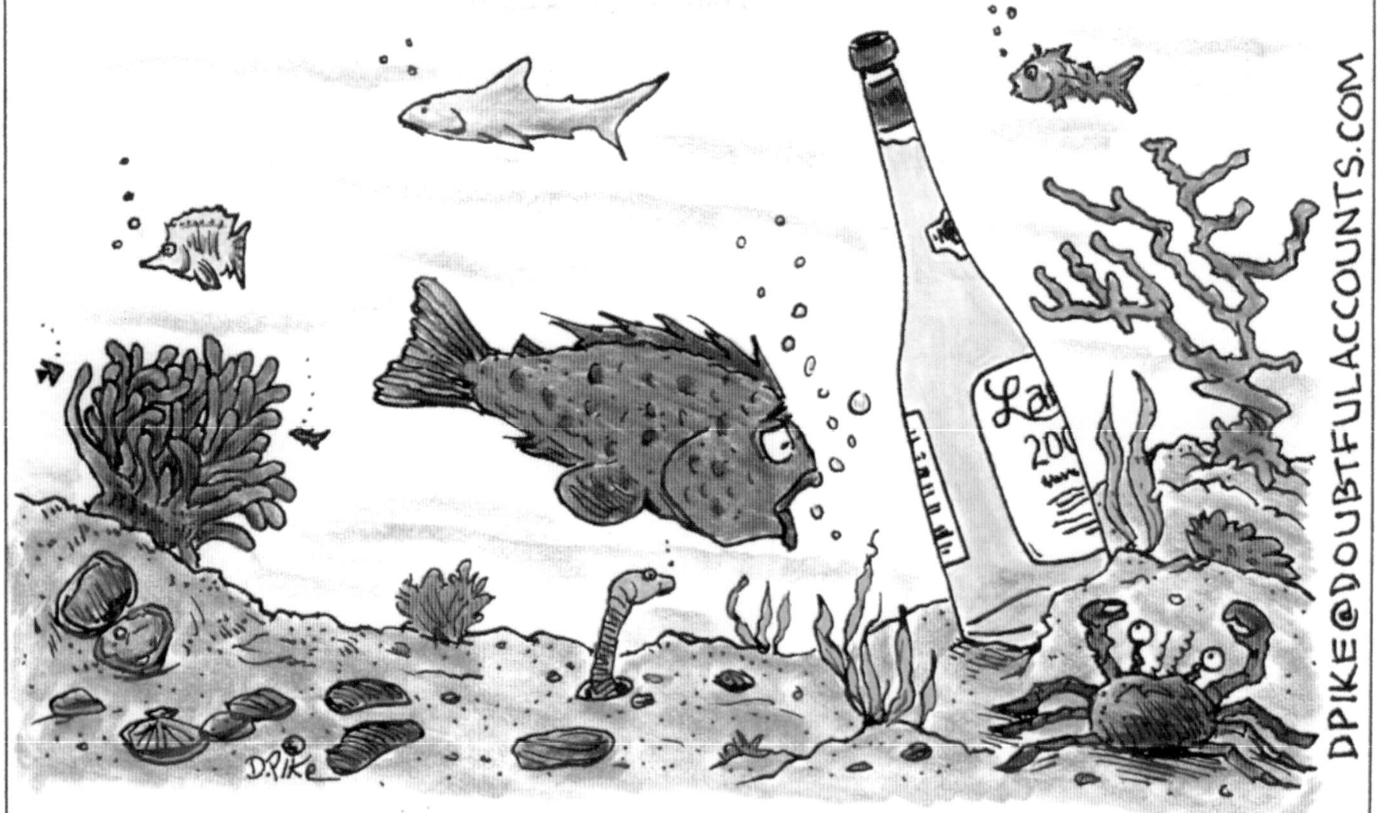
D.Pike
DPIKE@DOUBTFULACCOUNTS.COM

"Perfect with fish?"...That's sick!

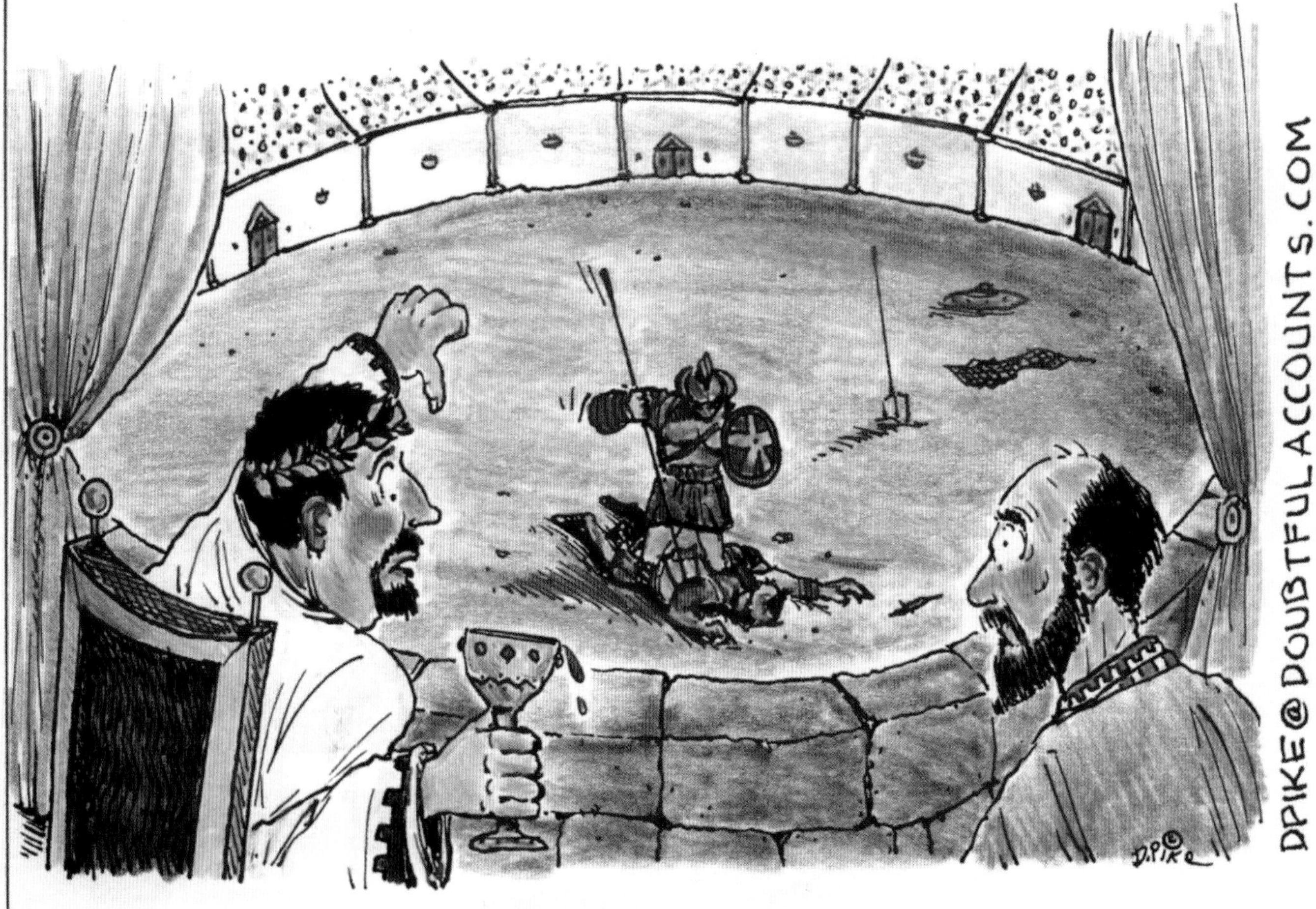
DPIKE@DOUBTFULACCOUNTS.COM
D.PIKE©

I meant the wine.

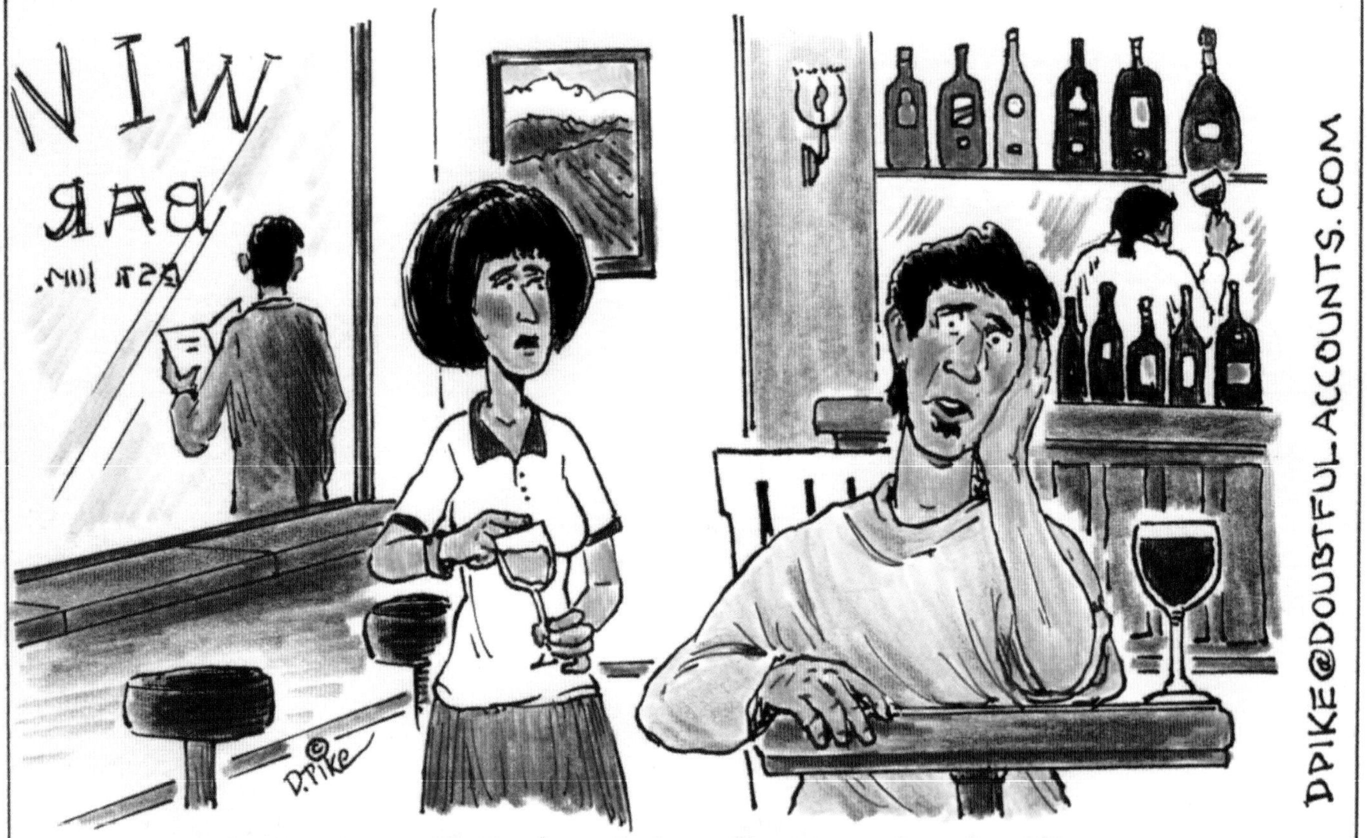
D.Pike
DPIKE@DOUBTFULACCOUNTS.COM

I nearly made it through culinary school selling wine books—then their library caught on.

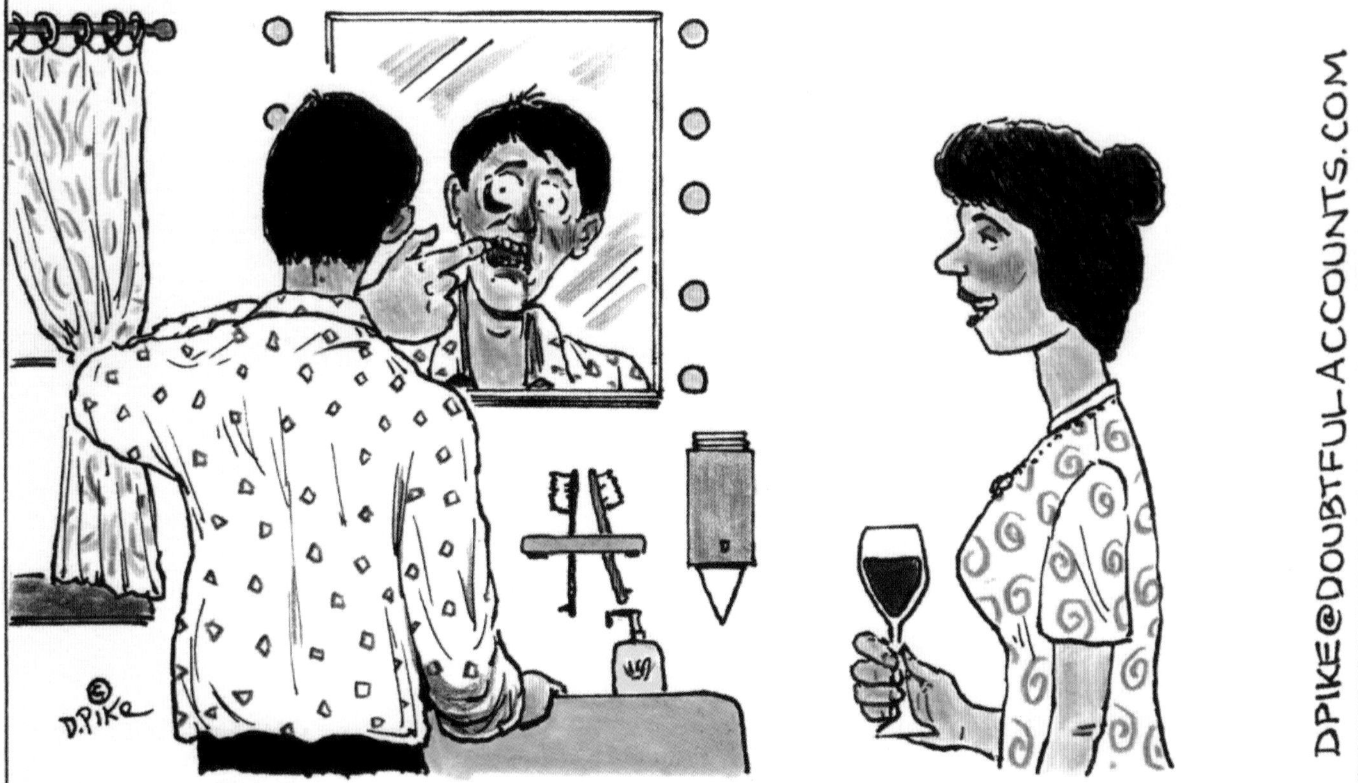
© D.Pike
DPIKE@DOUBTFULACCOUNTS.COM

Next time, make sure everyone knows what an oenophile is, before you go around introducing yourself as one.

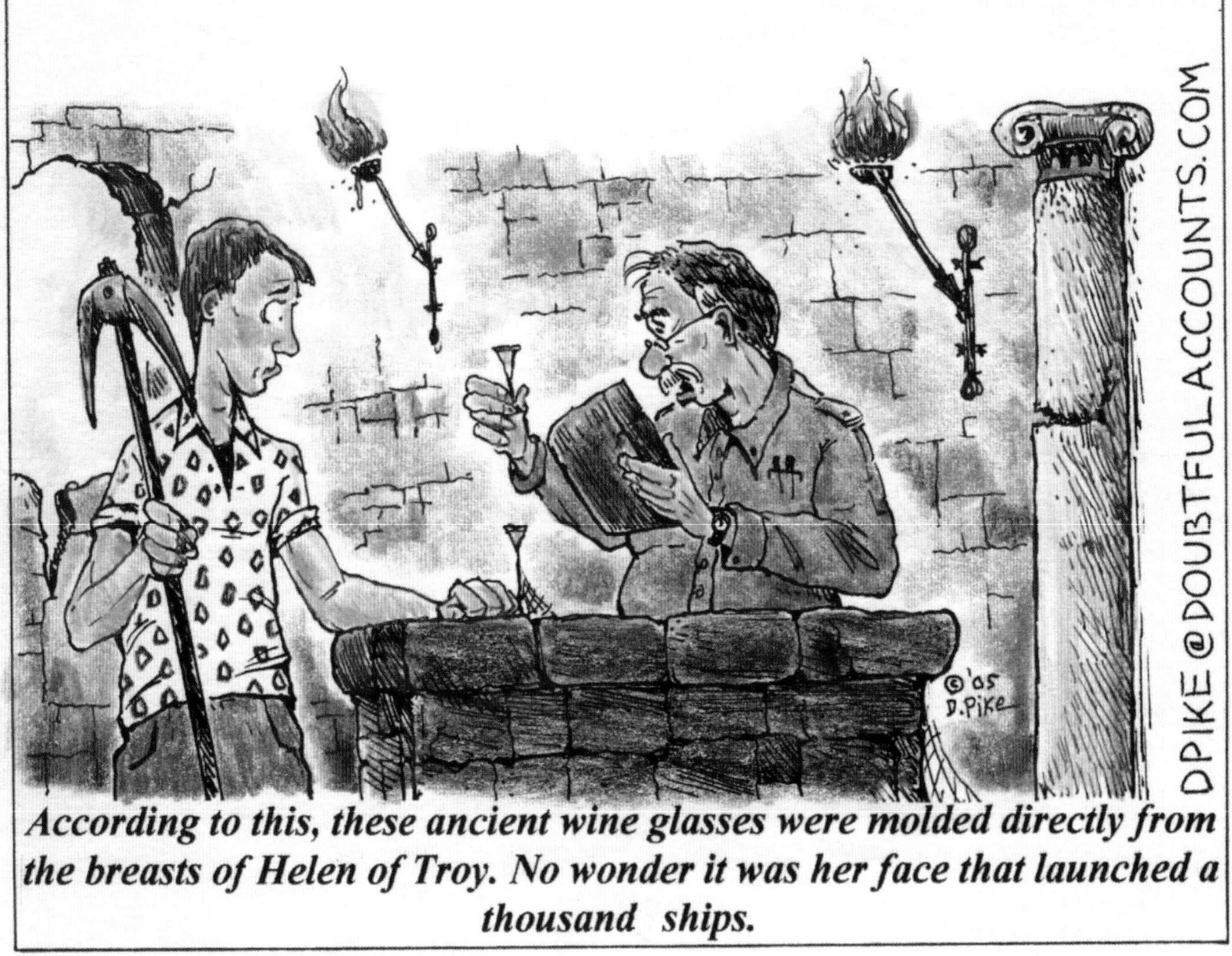
©'05
D.Pike
DPIKE@DOUBTFULACCOUNTS.COM

According to this, these ancient wine glasses were molded directly from the breasts of Helen of Troy. No wonder it was her face that launched a thousand ships.

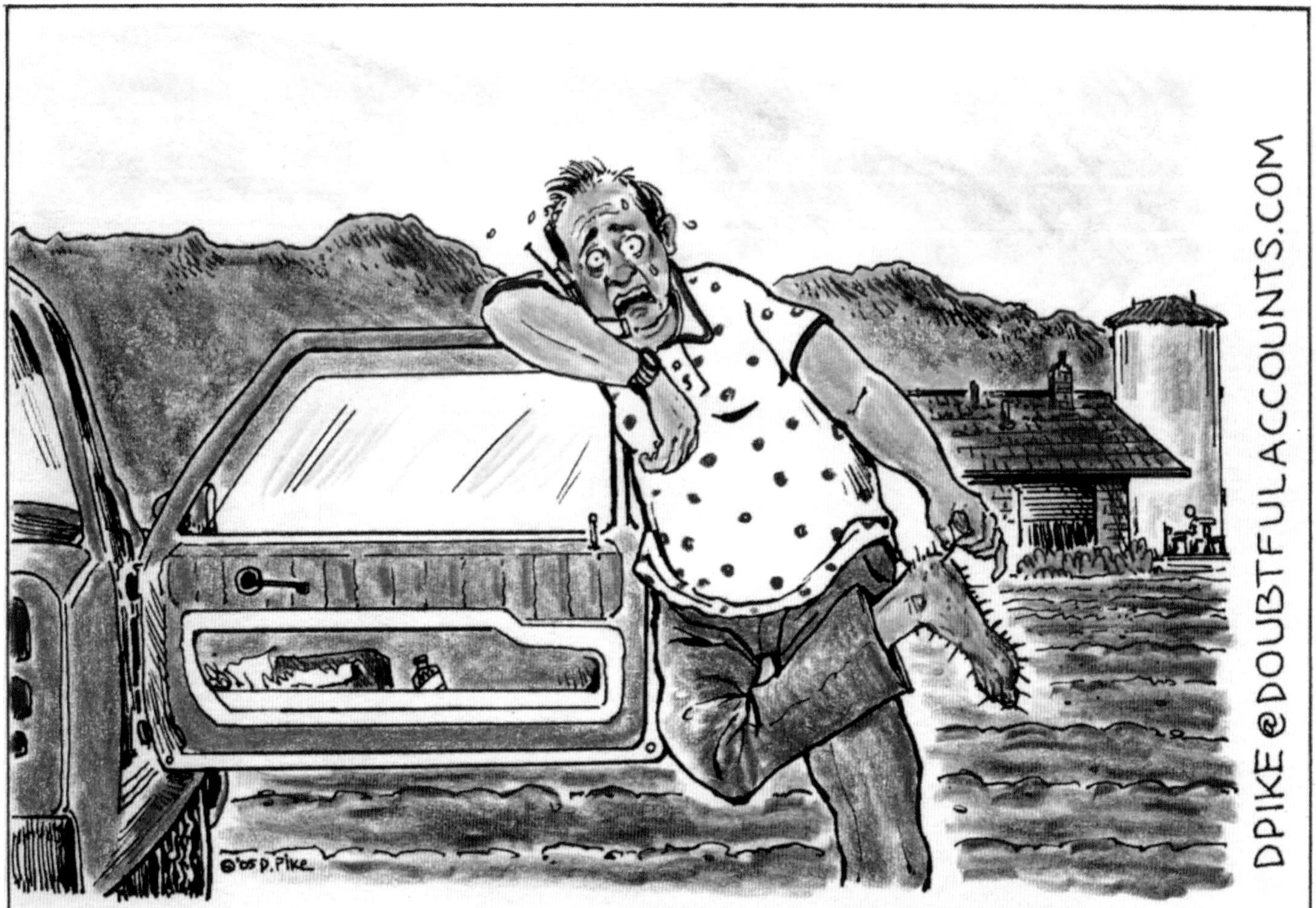
©'05 D. Pike
DPIKE @DOUBTFULACCOUNTS.COM

**Yeah, dear, I got the stomping job at the vineyard—
you didn't mention they make cactus wine!**

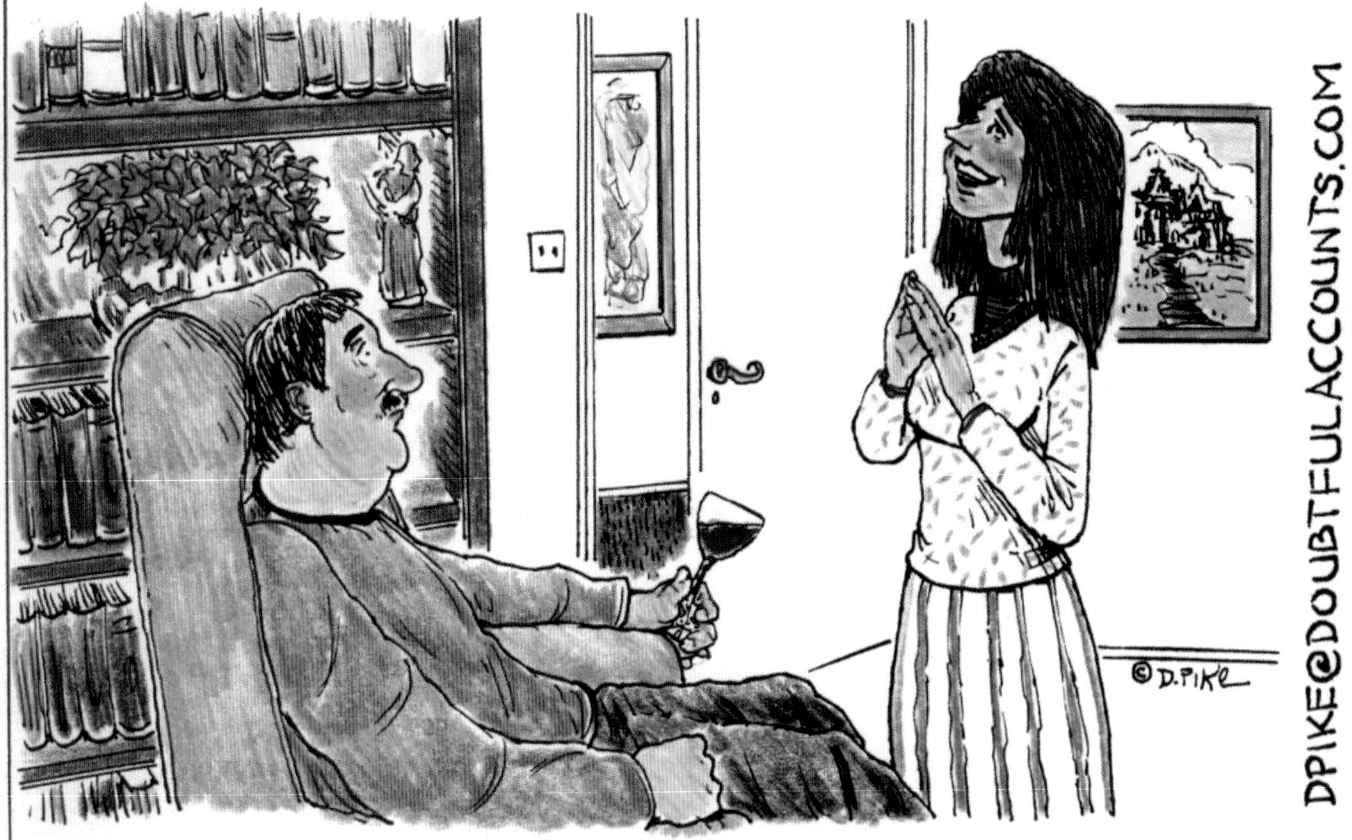
©D.PIKE
DPIKE@DOUBTFULACCOUNTS.COM

He's so-o-o-o sophisticated! We went to this French restaurant and he ordered a bottle of their finest wine—vin ordinaire!

Other Wine Humor Books by The Wine Appreciation Guild

Vine Lines: A cheery and humorous exploration of wine terminology

Vine Lines
A cheery and humorous exploration of wine terminology
Author Judy Valon Designer / Illustrator Roger Roberts
Dedicated to all wine lovers

Judy Valon, Illustrated by Roger Roberts
$14.95, ISBN 1-891267-93-0, Hardcover, 6X6", 96 pp

Illustrated by the well-known Australian cartoonist Roger Roberts, this charming, pocket-sized book explores the curious realm of wine terminology by creating a visual lexicon on the "far side" of a wine world where its language ("barnyard," "exotic nose") is taken literally. Sometimes brash, sometimes cute, Robert's work is always good for a sizable belly laugh. And in between these visual puns Judy Valon gives a serious and solid primer on enjoying wine, identify faults, proper entertaining and serving procedures, and, of course, the functioning definitions of common tasting terms.

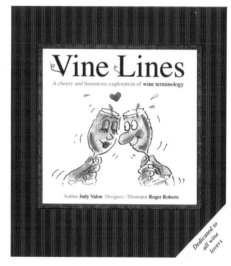

You're a Real Wine Lover When...

You're a Real Wine Lover When...

Bert Witte
$9.95, ISBN 1-891267- 25-6, Paperback, 8 1/2 x 7 inches, 72 pp

The famous Dutch cartoonist aims his sardonic brilliance at the seemingly simple pleasure of enjoying fermented grape juice. No facet of wine culture is spared. His drawings range from the elegant to the grotesque, distorting the human anatomy if necessary to make his razor-sharp point.

Other Books by The Wine Appreciation Guild

Africa Uncorked, John and Erica Platter
Armagnac, Charles Neal
The Bartender's Black Book, 9th ed. Stephen Kittredge Cunningham
Benefits of Moderate Drinking, Gene Ford
Biodynamic Wine Demystified, Nicholas Joly
California Brandy Drinks, Malcom R. Hebert
California Wine Drinks, William I. Kaufman
Champagne & Sparkling Wine Guide, Tom Stevenson
Cheese, Gabriella Ganugi
Chilean Wine Heritage, Rodrigo Alvarado
Chow! Venice, Shannon Essa and Ruth Edenbaum
The Commonsense Book of Wine, Leon D. Adams
Concepts in Wine Chemistry, Yair Margalit
Concepts in Wine Technology, Yair Margalit
Desert Island Wine, Miles Lambert-Gocs
Essential Guide to South African Wine, Elmari Swart
Favorite Recipes of California Winemakers
Fine Wine in Food, Patricia Ballard
Food & Wine Lovers' Guide to Portugal, Metcalfe and McWhirter
Ghost Wineries of the Napa Valley, Irene Whitford Haynes
The Global Encyclopedia of Wine, Edited by Peter Forrestal
Good Wine, Bad Language, Great Vineyards: Australia
Good Wine, Bad Language, Great Vineyards: New Zealand
Grape Man of Texas, McLeRoy and Renfro
Grappa, Ove Boudin
Greek Salad, Mile Lambert-Gocs
How and Why to Build a Wine Cellar, Richard Gold
Hungary, David Copp
I Supertuscan, Carlo Gambi
Icon: Art of the Wine Label, Jeffrey Caldewey and Chuck House
Imagery: Art for Wine, Bob Nugent
Journey Among the Great Wines of Sicily, Carlo Gambi
Making Sense of Wine Tasting, Alan Young
Napa Wine: A History, Charles L. Sullivan
The New Italy, Daniele Cernelli and Marco Sabellico

Northern Wine Works, 2nd ed. Thomas A. Plocher
Olive Oil, Leonardo Romanelli
Oregon Eco-Friendly Wine, Clive Michelsen
Pasta, Fabrizio Ungaro
Piedmont, Carlo Gambi
Portugal's Wines & Wine Makers, New Revised Ed., Richard Mason
Prosciutto, Carla Bardi
Red & White, Max Allen
Rich, Rare & Red, Ben Howkins
Rum, Dave Broom
Sauternes, Jeffrey Benson and Alastair McKenzie
The Science of Healthy Drinking, Gene Ford
Secrets of Chilean Cuisine, Robert Marin
Secrets of Patagonian Barbecue, Robert Marin
Secrets of Peruvian Cuisine, Emilio Peschiera
The Taste of Wine, Emile Peynaud
Tasting & Grading Wine, Clive Michelsen
Terroir, James E. Wilson
Tokaj, David Copp
Understanding Wine Technology, David Bird
The University Wine Course, Marian Baldy
The Wine Buyer's Record Book, Ralph Steadman
A Wine Growers' Guide, Philip M. Wagner
Wine Heritage, Dick Rosano
Wine in Everyday Cooking, Patricia Ballard
Wine, Food & the Good Life, Arlene Mueller and Dorothy Indelicato
Wine Investment for Portfolio Diversification, Mahesh Kumar
Wine Lovers Cookbook, Malcolm R. Herbert
Wine Marketing & Sales, Paul Wagner, Janeen Olsen, Liz Thach
Winery Technology & Operations, Yair Margalit
The Wines of Baja California, Ralph Amey
The Wines of France, Clive Coates
Woody's Liquid Kitchen, Hayden Wood
Zinfandel, Cathleen Francisco